SKI
MAGAZINE'S
TOTAL SKIING

(Bob Jonas)

SKI
MAGAZINE'S
TOTAL SKIING

Bob Jonas and Seth Masia

Illustrations by Ralph Harris

G. P. Putnam's Sons
New York

G. P. Putnam's Sons
Publishers Since 1838
200 Madison Avenue
New York, NY 10016

Library of Congress Cataloging-in-Publication Data

Jonas, Bob.
   Ski magazine's total skiing.

   1. Skis and skiing. I. Masia, Seth. II. Ski (New
York, N.Y.) III. Title. IV. Title: Total skiing.
GV854.J55   1987   796.93   87-10762
ISBN 0-399-13171-X

Typeset by Fisher Composition, Inc.

Printed in the United States of America
1 2 3 4 5 6 7 8 9 10

Acknowledgments

It was my parents, Bob Sr. and Frances Jonas, who first placed my brother John and me on skis some forty years ago. I thank them for more than just that early exposure to skiing—they gave me the urge to explore many things, including all the dimensions of skiing. John has shared with me the total ski experience over all these years. The pleasures of that relationship are inestimable. Nina, my daughter, much to my delight, takes equal pleasure in the total ski experience.

As a neophyte writer I owe much to my co-author, Seth Masia, and to the guidance of our editor at Putnam, Roger Scholl. They have given me much insight into the craft while reigning in my galloping muse. Seth has been great to work with and has become a good friend with whom I enjoy skiing. Ralph Harris, great friend, fine artist and skier, responded eagerly to our request that he illustrate the book. We could not have conveyed many of these concepts without his clear, potent drawings. My companion Claudine Martin tolerated my single-minded efforts in writing the book, its frustrations and pleasures. I thank her for that and for her constructive encouragement.

Skiers are a great and gregarious lot—fun to be with. For communicating to me their experience and pleasure in our sport in taped interviews, I thank Loren Adkins, Bob Rosso, Rick and Janet Barker, Bill Koch, Bob and Lori Sarchett, Jim and E. J. Holcomb, Leif Odmark, Mark Pearson, Kim Anderson, Joey Cordeau and Penelope Street. And an appreciation for all my friends over many years with whom I have shared the ski experience, especially those with whom I have known the backcountry trail. They are a special breed.

Gary Brettnacher and John Plummer responded immediately to photo requests. I appreciate very much the submissions of the other photographers whose credits appear in the book. Penelope Street and her sister, Pam, great skiers, appear on the title page photo. I thank them for their patience with me during our photo sessions on Mt. Baldy, and thank the Sun Valley Co. for providing us with the opportunity to shoot on the mountain.

The offices of the Professional Ski Instructors of America readily provided us with research materials.

Finally, a tribute to the sport itself. Total Skiing has enriched my life.

—Bob Jonas

First, thanks to my father, Bert, whose attempt to teach me tennis at an early age drove me to the woods and mountains; and thanks to Phyllis, my mother, who convinced me I could do anything I was willing to work at. Thanks to the editors and staff of *Ski* magazine, who provided the research facilities without which the book could not have been written, and particularly to editor Dick Needham, whose critique of the manuscript was invaluable.

A special note of gratitude is due to the writers who have gone before—especially to the historians. As source material, the following books and writers proved indispensable: Peter Lunn's recollections of his father, Sir Arnold, in *The Guinness Book of Skiing* (Guiness Superlatives Ltd, London); Leif Hovelsen's biography of his father Karl, *The Flying Norseman* (National Ski Hall of Fame Press, Ishpeming, Mich.); and Jakob Vaage's excellent work, especially the series of articles he did with Morten Lund that appeared in *Ski* under the heading "The Way It Was."

Finally, I should thank the oddly assorted bunch of characters who, over the years, taught me about the different worlds of skiing: Dick Bohr and Ferdl Aster, Pete Gorrel, Jacquie Metzger, Dick Dorworth, J.-P. Pascal, Alain Gaimard, Joe Bob Killy, Bob Jonas and Penelope Street, Franz Weber, Tom Lippert, the Poulsen boys, and Leroy Hill.

—Seth Masia

Contents

Among all recreational sports, cross-country track skiing is considered the most complete fitness exercise. *(John Plummer)*

Introduction
Total Skiing:
The Three Worlds

The universe of modern skiing offers the opportunity to discover three different worlds in one sport. We call the skier who explores each of these worlds a *Total Skier*. This book is meant as a guide to the entire cosmos of skiing, encouraging skiers to look at all three worlds as a way to acquire dynamic expert-level skills.

The three worlds are lift-served downhill skiing, cross-country skiing, and backcountry skiing. Each presents a distinct challenge to the adventurer who would be a total skier.

Lift-served downhill skiing is the most widely known form of the sport today. This is a world of machine-groomed mountain slopes served by lifts. When new snow falls overnight on a lift-served mountain, it remains in a natural state very briefly. On moderate terrain, it's rolled flat and smooth by snowcats. On steeper runs, skiers soon churn it up and pack it down. Where not enough new snow has fallen, high-pressure air and water hoses are used to create a dense blanket of easily packed snow. Lift-served downhill skiing is, 95 percent of the time, packed-snow skiing.

It's easier to learn and ski on packed surfaces than through untracked snow. The lifts swiftly convey one to the top of an astounding variety of terrain. Few sports challenge us the way downhill skiing does. The lift-served skier even has a choice of two very different techniques, Alpine and Telemark.

The free-heel cross-country downhill skier can glide down nearly any slope, but cross-country skiing offers other options. The cross-country skier can fly swiftly across gentle fields and rolling woodland, following a firm prepared track with the grace and rhythm of a fine athlete, or venture off the groomed trail through virgin snow at an easy, contemplative pace. Anyone who can walk can tour on cross-country skis. Touring is a peaceful, self-reliant, soul-satisfying sport. It depends on good snow and fresh air, not on lifts.

Backcountry skiing takes us into a remote world of total skiing adventure. It is an endless white wilderness of untouched snow and slopes, unknown valleys and far spaces. It is the grandeur and challenge of the unexpected. The backcountry skier may use both cross-country and downhill skis to ski flat valleys, rolling hills, steep mountainsides and ridgecrests. In the wilderness, the skier relies on good sense and deep knowledge of snow, weather and terrain to find the

Cross-country tour skiing is a contemplative outing into winter's beauty and silence. *(Bob Jonas)*

safe route and secure camp.

Total skiing is a new idea, born with the transformation of the ski from a crude, heavy wooden runner into a beautiful, lively instrument made of light, dynamic space-age materials. Today, while there is a ski for every kind of snow and terrain, certain skis are so versatile as to open entire worlds to the intrepid skier.

The skimeister of an earlier era, proficient in cross-country and downhill techniques, was a complete skier in his time. But time has changed the sport enormously. Today's Total Skier has access to a broad variety of lift-served, groomed-track and wilderness terrain that would astonish the skimeister. New, more efficient skiing techniques have

evolved, in parallel with modern equipment, so that the Total Skier can go places and do things on skis the skimeister could not have imagined.

Who are the Total Skiers? Relatively few people have explored, let alone mastered, all three worlds of skiing. Largely this is because of time constraints. An important marketing study commissioned by the ski industry in 1985 identified the skiing aficionado as someone who skis twelve days or more each winter. A twelve-day skier hardly has the opportunity in a single season to sample skiing's cornucopia. If you can ski only twelve days a year, you might very well feel obligated to maximize your mileage by riding lifts at a popular resort.

But there are broader possibilities out there. The Total Skier, pushing back the limits, has the entire white world, a world of endless skiing filled with fresh snow, sunny days and good friends. Co-authors Seth Masia and Bob Jonas met with a few friends at the edge of a white wilderness and toured to a mountain hut, a cozy shelter nestled in pine woods.

Last season we toured higher, above timberline to the sheer face of a soaring peak. The run back to the hut was downhill through broad powderfields. Another day we established a track, running successive loops across a frozen Alpine lake.

Back in town, at the foot of a great lift-served mountain, we closed out the backcountry trip with a fine five-course meal and a steaming session in the hot tub. In the morning, the group worked out the remaining muscle kinks (and hangovers) in a couple of vigorous laps of the cross-country track. Lunch found us all at the summit of the lift-served mountain, lounging in the sun and swapping stories with ski bums and jet-setters with accents from around the world. Then it was an afternoon of exhilarating Alpine skiing. In a few days we had sampled the entire universe of total skiing.

Join us as we explore this universe in detail. Skiing today is an open sport of endless possibility, easy to learn yet so varied and vast that you can continue to learn new skiing skills your whole life long. Come with us and become a Total Skier.

Skiing is a world of endless adventure. *(Gary Brettnacher)*

All kinds of people used crude skis to traverse the snowy countryside for thousands of years before the advent of skiing as a sport.

1
The Early Experience

Bertram Bernard, at age sixty-two, learned to ski last winter. He flew out from New York to Squaw Valley, California, bringing along the cross-country skis he had been given for Christmas. He had been playing tennis and riding his bicycle regularly, so he was in good shape. In spite of the altitude, he was kicking and gliding around the trail network very happily after only a single day of lessons. He was hooked.

But Bernard discovered he liked to stay on the easier, more level trails. His skis had no steel edges; while they were light and maneuverable, they tended to skitter sideways when he got going too fast on the downhill sections.

Bernard had just discovered the driving force in the evolution of skiing: the difficulty in making cross-country equipment behave itself in steep terrain. Until very recently, the technology simply did not exist to build skis and boots that would handle easily both running across the flats and whizzing downhill.

Because of this, two separate styles of skiing developed: With the first, one simply plunges downhill, joyously following the mountain where it will take you; the other, while not ideal for controlled downhill skiing, offers the freedom to stride uphill and across level terrain.

Traditionally, the practical, versatile climbing-and-running technique is called Nordic (cross-country) skiing, because it was developed in the Scandinavian countries. The purely downhill style of skiing is called Alpine, because it was invented to deal with the steep and difficult terrain in the high Alps of Austria, Switzerland and France.

Today, the two styles have become distinctly separate. Partly this is because the two styles require superficially different skills. In general, we consider any style of skiing that allows the heel to lift off the ski in a natural stride to be Nordic and any style that locks the heel of the boot down for more secure control of the ski, Alpine. But the two styles began as one, and are really inseparable sides of the same coin. Skiing is a single sport, not two. The Total Skier is comfortable with his heel free or locked. He or she is a citizen of both worlds.

HOW SKIING ORIGINATED

For thousands of years, farmers, herders, hunters and warriors from Norway to Siberia traversed their rolling hills and steppes by sliding on skis. Their skis were crudely carved from single planks of wood, their "boots" simple leggings of cloth, leather or even bark. The foot was held to the ski with a leather strap over the ball of the foot, so the ski behaved like a floppy seven-foot-long sandal. With this rig you had to keep shuffling along— a vigorous backward kick in the modern cross-country style could pull your foot right out of the binding. Skiing downhill was possible only because the skis, sealed against water with pine tar, didn't glide very well. In fact, the term ski had little of the gliding connotation it has for us today. Pronounced then and now as "shee" by the Norse, it was simply the same word they used for "shoe." A ski was a snow-shoe. It was a purely utilitarian device, the only reasonable form of winter transportation.

It's not clear when the first ski races were organized in Norway and Sweden, but it was probably in the 1820s. As early as the eighteenth century, the King of Sweden is known to have offered prizes for skiing expertise to his troops, in the same spirit that he rewarded expert marksmanship. But by the middle of the nineteenth century, local farmboys competed with one another in running and jumping on skis.

The first really reliable records of skiing as a sport focus on one Elling Baekken, a farmer from Honefoss, who in 1866 skied fifty miles to Christiania (now called Oslo), to show off his skill to the skiers of Norway's capital city. The following year, the local skiers organized a race, which would eventually grow to be the world-famous Holmenkollen event. But the very first running of the Christiania race was crude. The mile-long course included a downhill bit, with a bump designed to throw racers into the air. The resulting jump was about 15 feet long. On simple rough skis, with toe-strap bindings, the downhill was a frightening prospect.

Enter Sondre Norheim, skiing's first genius. Like most great champions in skiing, Norheim succeeded by inventing a new, more efficient skiing technique, as well as better equipment to make his new style easier. In the process, he helped to create downhill skiing out of the elements of cross-country, making it possible for skiing to become a worldwide phenomenon.

Born in 1825 in Morgedal, a village in Norway's Telemark region, Norheim became a local ski-racing hero. He excelled in ski-jumping as well. In order to better control his skis on steep slopes and jumps, Norheim invented a stiffer binding, with a stout cord that passed behind the heel of his leather workboots. The cord not only held his shoes securely in their toe-straps, but also reinforced the boots laterally so the heels wouldn't twist sideways off the skis. While his heel would still lift, Norheim could now advance his foot forward and cock the other back, tipping the skis onto one edge. In the crouched landing position after a long ski jump, edging the skis this way produced a graceful controlled turn, and Norheim found he could ski safely to a stop from much higher speeds than his peers could manage. Like all his friends, Norheim carved his own skis from single planks of wood, but he carved them with a narrow waist, giving the ski a gentle

The earliest ski bindings were fashioned from leather.

hourglass profile. Now, when he tilted the ski on edge, it steered itself around in a much shorter turn.

With his maneuverability, Norheim beat all comers. In 1868, already an old man of forty-two, he journeyed to Christiania and won the race there handily. The locals were astounded. They dubbed his turn the "telemark." Among the skiers he taught it to were Mikkel and Torjus Hemmestveit. They invented a second turn, in which the skis were held roughly parallel and edged in the same direction. The "Christiania" resulted in a quick turn that could be used to scrub off (or slow down) speed going downhill. The Hemmestveits' "Christie" proved to be the key to the success of skiing in Central Europe.

In the Alps, as in the North, skiing as transportation had been in existence for a long time—at least 500 years in the Julian Alps, where Austria, Italy and Yugoslavia meet. But the development of downhill skiing, purely as sport, awaited the growth of "Alpinism" and the development of the railroads. Alpinism means simply mountain climbing. No one climbed mountains for fun until the budding Romantic movement began to draw vigorous young men of leisure into the high country at the close of the eighteenth century. Mont Blanc, Europe's highest peak, was first climbed in 1786 by Dr. Peccard, a physician who lived in its shadow. But the classic age of Alpine climbing coincided with the height of British power in the Victorian era. It was in 1865 that Edward Whymper made the first ascent of the Matterhorn.

Whymper and his friends were not just great adventurers. They were writers, too. Their books, climbing and trekking guides to the great Alpine valleys, drew crowds of summer vacationers up the new railway lines to towns like Chamonix, Zermatt and St. Anton. By 1880 many tiny farming communities boasted luxury hotels. Inevitably, guests wanted something to do at these palaces during the winter months. They tobogganed and skated and played cards. They were ripe for skiing.

A great Norwegian adventurer-writer named Fridtjof Nansen in 1888 led five men on a lightning six-week crossing of the Greenland ice cap on skis. He wrote a book about the trip in 1890 called *By Skis Across Greenland*. The book fired the imaginations of Central European mountaineers. One of Nansen's fans was a thirty-four-year-old Austrian gymnast named Matthias Zdarsky. In 1890 Zdarsky had recently taken up a bohemian and hermetic life in the mountain village of Lilienfeld. Surrounded by snowy hillsides, Zdarsky sent away for a pair of skis. When they arrived at the railway station he found he couldn't use them. The leather bindings were too flexible to allow climbing back up the hill to his house. At 294 cm, the skis were too long to make it around the corners when he tried to traverse. Zdarsky didn't know how to kick-turn, and the skis were too long to permit it anyway. He had to walk home, skis on his shoulder.

It's easy to imagine Zdarsky's frustration. Almost every beginner finds his skis clumsy and overwhelming during the first few hours. But Zdarsky was stubborn. Fiercely independent and self-reliant, he was intrigued with the concept of skiing, and was undeterred by the fact that the only existing skis were completely unsuitable for use on steep terrain. If no one else could help him learn how to use the skis, he'd teach himself. Zdarsky proved to be a classic bootstrap inventor. In complete isolation, over the

Early downhill skiers had to rely on a long pole to control their descent. *(Sun Valley Co.)*

course of the next six winters, he invented everything he needed to negotiate the steep hillsides of the Alps.

To turn his skis accurately, Zdarsky built a binding that was even stiffer than Norheim's. He lopped two feet off the tails of his skis, bringing them down to a more manageable seven-foot length. Finally—and most important—he invented the "stem," and with it the ability to begin a stable turn no matter what the terrain or snow conditions. To stem a ski is simply to push its tail outward, so that the two skis form a V. If you then stand on the displaced ski, it will turn in the direction it's pointed. Zdarsky found he could stem the downhill ski to point himself uphill, thus slowing his speed. And he could stem the uphill ski, thus beginning to turn down and back across the hill in the other direction.

Because he lived alone, and far from other skiers, it wasn't until 1896 that Zdarsky realized he could do things on skis no one else in Austria could do. Even this late, skiers—Zdarsky included—depended on a single stout pole for balance and propulsion on the flat. The pole was also used as a brake when it came time to slide downhill. If he hadn't been so serious about skiing, Zdarsky might have burst out laughing the first time he saw a group of skiers descending a gentle slope, riding their poles like so many hobbyhorses. Instead, Zdarsky the pragmatist ran home and wrote a book. Published in Germany in the fall of 1896, the *Lilienfelder Skilauftechnik*—in English, the Lilienfeld Ski-Running Technique—taught everyone who would read it how to control speed with the skis alone, simply by stemming and turning.

The book was a sensation in a region where mountaineers customarily climbed to the summit on skis—and walked back down, because they didn't know any other way to get home safely. Zdarsky the hermit became, overnight, Zdarsky the guru. The railroads put on special excursions to Lilienfeld so that Viennese skiers could learn to stem under Zdarsky's supervision.

Stubborn as ever, Zdarsky proved to be a strict disciplinarian. Perhaps he needed to be in order to deal with the crowds. In particular, his rigidity proved useful when, during World War I, he was called upon to teach thousands of soldiers to ski. But his insistence that there was one way to do it—his way—helped to splinter the world of skiing once the Norwegians got wind of what he was doing. It was here that the deep crevasse first opened between Alpine and Nordic skiing.

Zdarsky had not set himself up in opposition to traditional ski-running; he had simply figured out a way to use Norwegian equipment on steeper hillsides. But some Scandinavians were infuriated to learn that an Austrian was changing their sport.

For Scandinavians, skiing had, in the half century since Norheim's arrival in Christiania, become the Norse religion. Norwegians, in particular, reacted with horror again and again to innovations produced by outsiders. Much later, for example, when the Englishman Arnold Lunn sought to introduce downhill rac-

Arlberg ski technique in the early days of Alpine skiing.

ing to the international competition calendar early in the 1920s, one Norwegian official asked, "How would you like it if I tried to change the rules of cricket?" "I wish to heaven you would," Lunn had replied. When American and Central European companies introduced fiberglass cross-country skis in the 1970s, Scandinavian factories resisted abandoning wood right to the point of bankruptcy. And when the American racer Bill Koch beat the world by skating around cross-country courses in the early 1980s, Scandinavian officials fought tooth and nail for the next five years to get the technique outlawed.

Had Zdarsky adopted a conciliatory tone, the Nordic/Alpine split might never have occurred. He might have sat down with his Norwegian critics and said, "You guys are great. I figured out all this stuff by reading Nansen and emulating Norheim. Here's what I'm doing. Let's go skiing and then have some schnapps." But that's not how his mind worked. Zdarsky was offended that anyone might consider his technique—and his own mastery of it—anything other than marvelous. In reaction to the storm from the north, he even changed the name of his book, dropping the word *"lauf"*—which means running, Norwegian style—in favor of the word *"fahr"*—which means riding, and implies downhill gliding.

Hannes Schneider, a younger disciple of Zdarsky, took advantage of the new rigidly bound boot heel to combine the Hemmestveits' Christie with Zdarsky's stem. The resulting stem christie became the foundation of Schneider's Arlberg ski technique, which would allow thousands of urban adventurers to learn to ski without ever venturing upon a cross-country track. Another helpful innovation Schneider used was the steel edge. Invented by the Austrian Rudolph Lettner to help wooden skis last longer, steel edges were accepted immediately by Alpine skiers because they provided skate-like control on hard-frozen snow.

Despite their adoption of the christie, most Central European skiers came to feel they owed nothing to the ungracious Scandinavians. As the chasm between the two kinds of skiing widened, Alpine and Nordic competitions developed as separate, nonoverlapping sports. Only in America did college ski coaches, drawing on the melting pot of Norwegian, Austrian, Swiss and French influences, insist that their athletes ski four events: slalom, downhill, cross-country and jumping.

SKIING IN AMERICA

Skiing began in the Americas with the arrival of Norwegian immigrants. The first Norwegian skiers turned up in Illinois and Wisconsin as early as 1836.

But the first organized ski races in the Americas were held not in the Midwest, but at the western rim of the country. When gold was discovered at Sutter's Mill, sailors jumped ship in San Francisco to head for the Sierras. The Norwegians among them weathered the winter of 1849 with considerably more relish than their comrades. They made skis and organized races. In the Sierra foothills, those races were of necessity downhills— the first organized downhill races in the world. Because sizable cash prizes were awarded in races between rival mining camps, these were also the first professional ski races. We know of race meetings as early as 1853, in Onion Valley, California; the following year, miners were racing, at breakneck speed, in mass-start downhills with no control gates. These were straight runs (a straight run without turns is referred to in skiing as a schuss), and they were performed on 15-foot planks with simple, pre-Norheim toe-straps. The earliest race timing for which records survive was a challenge: on February 5, 1863, Norwegian miner Andrew Jacobsen, of Sierra Hills, California, skied a half-mile course in under 20 seconds, to beat Ike Zent of Whisky Diggings. The prize: $100. If the time and the distance were measured accurately, Jacobsen averaged over 90 mph. His skis had been waxed carefully (the Norwegians back home wouldn't discover ski wax for another twenty years).

The American long boards may not have been equipped with Norheim bindings or quick-turning sidecuts, but they were good enough for purely utilitarian purposes. Intrepid skiers throughout the West, from Idaho to New Mexico, carried the mail to remote mining towns winter after winter. The most famous of the skiing mail carriers were Snowshoe Thompson (born John Tostensen Rui, in Telemark), and "Father" John Dyer.

In the 1880s, thousands of Scandinavian families came over to homestead—and among them were men like Mikkel and Torjus Hemmestveit, John Hauge, even Sondre Norheim himself. These four, among the thousands, happened to be past winners of the Holmenkollen King's Cup. Victory in sport did not, in those days, guarantee prosperity; even national heroes had to emigrate simply to feed their families. Not all were successful. Norheim, like Snowshoe Thompson, died penniless, in 1897.

But many Norwegians did prosper—enough, at least, to devote leisure time to their sport. Norwegian immigrants founded the first Eastern ski club in Berlin, New Hampshire, in 1872. By 1888 some dozen clubs had been organized in towns west of Lake Michigan, and the first cross-country races were held in St. Paul in January of 1887. The following year 6,000 spectators and 200 competitors showed up for a meet in Eau Claire. These were sophisticated skiers, using modern Norheim-style equipment, able to jump, turn and run on their skis. Like the early Christiania races, the cross-country courses included some high-speed downhill sections, and skiers were expected to enter both cross-country and jumping competitions.

A pivotal figure of the period was Karl Hovelsen, of Christiania. Born in 1877, Hovelsen was a short, wiry firecracker, who skied to championships in both cross-country and jumping. He won the King's Cup in 1903. In 1905, Hovelsen, an unemployed mason, shipped to America, where he anglicized his name to Carl Howelsen.

He found plenty of work as a bricklayer in Chicago, and plenty of skiing, too. By November, he and twenty-seven other Chicago-area Norwegians had founded the Norge Ski Club, and Howelsen was put in charge of building a ski jump. He found a site on the banks of the Fox River, where the club soon built a lodge, and regular competition began in 1907. Within a year, the Norge Club jumping meets would draw 10,000 spectators. Part of the reason was that Howelsen had become, during the summer of 1907, the most famous skier in the world.

He did it by accepting an offer to jump for the circus. His act was the center-ring attraction that year for the Barnum & Bailey "Greatest Show on

Earth." For Howelsen it was a piece of cake to tear down a greased ramp and hop 40 feet to land on a stretched-canvas platform. But the circus paid him the astronomical sum of $200 a week, and by the time his season ended (with a sprained shoulder, the result of a fall from a ladder), Howelsen felt financially secure. Turning the circus job over to a ski-jumping friend, he returned to Chicago, but not before showing some 2.5 million people during the sixteen-state circus tour a ski jump for the first time.

Howelsen eventually moved to Denver, where he found masonry work, and spectacular mountains for a strong skier within an hour's run. Howelsen and his friends began making overnight ski tours to settlements near the Continental Divide. At Hot Sulphur Springs Howelsen stumbled across a Swiss hotel-keeper named John Peyer. Like Swiss hotel-keepers back home, Peyer was enthusiastic about selling hotel rooms even in the depth of winter. To that end he had already helped to organize a winter festival in Hot Sulphur Springs, featuring toboggan races, skating and snowshoeing events. When Howelsen and friends skied into town, Peyer threw wide his doors and added ski races to the program.

Howelsen instantly became the father of recreational skiing in Colorado. In late 1913 Denver's Park Board had approved construction of a ski jump and race course at Inspiration Point, and Howelsen, along with half a dozen Norwegian friends, was giving lessons to all comers. The local papers reported that huge crowds—up to 20,000—turned out for his jumping exhibitions, and he was not above other high-speed stunts, like skiing down a toboggan slide at 70 mph. The following month Howelsen paid his first visit to Steamboat Springs, a tiny farming and ranching village in the remote Yampa Valley. He fell in love with the place.

Within a year he had bought a small ranch near Steamboat. Howelsen was affable, loquacious, enthusiastic and, to outward appearances, absolutely fearless. Kids found the combination irresistible, and before the first winter ended he had every child old enough to walk following him around on skis. Howelsen showed the local carpenters how to build a ski jump—a big one. By 1916 world records were being set on Howelson's Hill. Local skiers trained by Howelsen began showing up in the record books, and Norwegian champions like Ragnar Omtvedt journeyed to Steamboat to defend their own records. The first 200-foot jump made anywhere was made at Howelsen, and it was a doubly satisfying accomplishment because it was the first world record set by a native-born American, twenty-three-year-old Henry Hall. The year was 1917.

By the time he had sold his ranch and moved back to Norway to get married, Howelsen had inspired two generations of snowbound Coloradans to turn skier, and Steamboat had become world famous as a capital of Nordic skiing. By this time, of course, Alpine-style skiing was in full bloom in Europe, and it would shortly cross to America.

In 1921, English travel agent Arnold Lunn (later knighted Sir Arnold for his contributions to skiing) developed slalom racing. Lunn and his father had been organizing ski trips to the Alps for years, and the downhill obstacle course that is the slalom—a race around poles set vertically in the snow—was meant to be another diversion for his clients. The format was instantly popular, from

Chamonix to the Arlberg. It took two years for word to reach Dartmouth College, where the first intercollegiate ski meet had been held, but the moment he read about the new race, Charles Albert Proctor, faculty adviser of the Outing Club, was out cutting saplings for slalom poles. The year was 1923, and Dartmouth, by holding the first Alpine race in North America, earned the right to be considered the birthplace of American Alpine skiing.

In 1926, the first American Alpine downhill race was held at Mt. Moosilauke, New Hampshire. Downhill racing was still closely related to cross-country racing. The racers had to climb to the top of the mountain, usually on their racing skis. The boot heel was not yet fastened securely to the top of the ski (that would happen in 1933, with the introduction of the Kandahar binding). The downhill course itself was simply a logging road, a narrow twisting trail descending through the hardwood forest. There were enough flat and uphill sections that a skier needed to be able to run on his skis as well as to glide. Racers expected to fall and to get back up to complete the course; if you could run a course without falling, you stood to win the race by a margin of minutes. With no telecommunications between start and finish, the officials simply synchronized two clocks, then carried one to the top of the mountain for the start. Racers were started at prearranged one-minute intervals, in much the way cross-country races were run.

Slalom races were much easier to organize. At least the timer at the bottom could see the starting gate, and could simply wave a flag to signal that he was starting his stop watch. Spectators could see the entire course, and, of course, it was a shorter hike for racers to reach the top.

In 1928 Arnold Lunn, with the Austrian Hannes Schneider, organized the first major international race, the Arlberg-Kandahar, so named because the British General Lord Roberts of Kandahar donated the trophy.

By the mid-thirties, with rope tows springing up on hillsides in Quebec, Vermont and New Hampshire, the railroads were ready to boost skiing. Averell Harriman, the young chairman of the Union Pacific Railroad, noted that hundreds of would-be skiers rode trains from New York and Boston up to New England farms, just to ride the rickety rope tows. These were crude, homemade devices powered by Ford motor cars put up on blocks for the winter. The rope was simply wrapped around a rear wheel and the engine cranked up. Harriman figured he could do better.

He hired experts, beginning with Austrian Count Felix Schaffgotsch. The count explored the Union Pacific's high-mountain lines throughout the West for six weeks before settling on Ketchum, Idaho, as the site for the railroad's million-dollar hotel. Harriman also moved fast. Schaffgotsch arrived in Ketchum in January of 1936; the hotel and ski hill were open for business in December. The most notable Union Pacific innovation was the chairlift, designed by railroad engineer Jim Curran, based on aerial cables he had built in South America for hauling bananas down to the docks. The new resort opened with two chairs: one on Dollar Mountain (still the area's beginner hill) and one on Proctor Mountain, named for Dartmouth racer Charles N. Proctor, son of the Dartmouth skiing club adviser, and one of Harriman's hired experts.

The resort was named Sun Valley, a public relations ploy to draw devotees of the sun to snow country. The Hollywood hoopla accompanying the grand opening was a fitting fanfare: Sun Valley was a milestone. With the creation of the resort, skiing became a national sport. By 1936 all the important inventions were in place: the locked-heel binding, steel edges, the Seelos parallel turn, the Arlberg method of ski instruction—even *Ski* magazine, which published its first issue in January of that year.

With the invention of high-speed uphill transportation, the split between Nordic and Alpine skiing widened. No longer was it necessary for Alpine skiers even to learn how to climb, or to equip themselves for it. Ski designers began to specialize: the cross-country racer and jumper had no need for steel edges, for instance. The concept of the complete skier existed only in collegiate ski competitions, where skiers were expected to be four-event men. To be a skimeister, or overall champ, an American college skier had to do well in jumping, cross-country, downhill and slalom. As equipment became even more refined and competition keener, college skiers became specialists after the mid-sixties. It's ironic that the all-around skier is an American notion. In Europe, Scandinavian resistance to Alpine competition meant that there never was a combined event for Nordic and Alpine skiing in international competition. Nordic Combined was, and remains, an event for cross-country racers and jumpers; Alpine combined began as a downhill and slalom, and today has returned to that format (after a period in which giant slalom also counted). One champion skier—Norway's Birger Ruud—won gold medals in both downhill and

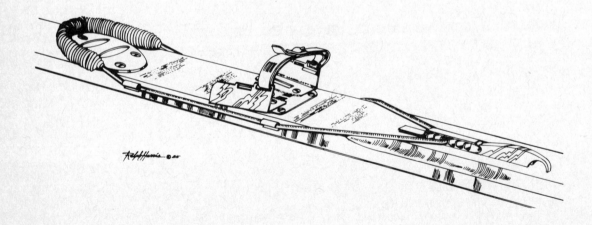

An Alpine ski binding, circa 1940.

jumping, but only in North America did a strong tradition of all-around skiing develop. There were some remarkable American skimeisters—men like Gordy Wren, a world-class jumper from Steamboat Springs, who also qualified for the Olympic team in cross-country, slalom and downhill.

It's appropriate, therefore, that a new kind of skimeister, the Total Skier, and a new concept, Total Skiing, would begin in the Rockies with the rebirth of the Norwegian telemark turn in the Seventies as a tool for exploring the backcountry. Only in America could the Scandinavian and Alpine traditions merge into a practical, universal, multifaceted single sport.

(Bob Jonas)

2
The Modern Experience

Sun Valley set the pattern for the great North American ski resorts, which were to arise after World War II: Aspen, Mont Tremblant, Squaw Valley, Stowe, Alta, Crystal, Mammoth, Jackson Hole, Lake Louise, Sugarloaf, Winter Park, Sugarbush, Vail, Steamboat, Park City, Waterville, Crested Butte, Telluride, Whistler . . .

The United States alone claims over 650 lift-served ski areas, and they're as various as the mountains on which they're built. One way to categorize ski resorts is by elevation and snow conditions, lumping the small hills of the Midwest together, followed by the 3,000-to 5,000-foot mountains of New England and New York, the 8,000- to 10,000-foot peaks of the Northern Sierra and Cascade ranges, and the 10,000- to 12,000-foot monsters of the Rockies and High Sierra. According to this hierarchy, higher is better.

But that's not quite how skiers see things when it actually comes time to pack up the car and take off for the weekend. From the point of view of the city-dwelling skier, ski areas fall into three broad types—a Mom-and-Pop ski area, a weekend ski resort, and a destination ski resort—depending on their proximity to cities. This is an important way of looking at ski areas if only be-

cause, according to the U.S. Census Bureau, 76 percent of Americans live in metropolitan areas.

Fortunately, in those geographical areas that receive snow, most cities are within an hour's drive of some kind of ski hill. Such a skiing location may often be a 500-foot nubbin or riverbank with a couple of surface lifts and a warming hut. These places usually got started when a farmer got talked into running a rope tow up some slope that was too steep to plow. The land is usually still in the family. The Mom-and-Pop ski area survives on a steady diet of new skiers, which it attracts by making skiing convenient. It offers night skiing, so people can come skiing after work. It advertises Wednesday as Ladies' Day, to entice housewives to come out for the day. It makes special deals with church groups, school clubs and the city YMCA to teach the kids to ski. The ski school is busy from ten AM to ten PM.

A Mom-and-Pop hill may have a chairlift or two, but it's more likely to have several T-bars. More often than not, Pop is responsible for keeping the lifts running and supervising the busy rental shop, while Mom keeps the hot chocolate flowing and the hot dogs warm, and looks after the books. The P.A. system plays a steady diet of Strauss waltzes beginning at dusk, when the parking lot begins to fill up. A couple of floodlights throw the moguls into stark relief. As the temperature plummets, skiers grow more sociable. There may be time to get in twenty runs between six and ten PM.

Roughly half of America's 650 ski areas may fall into the Mom-and-Pop category, and it's likely that three-quarters of all skiers got started at these places.

Once hooked on night skiing, a city skier may begin spending weekends at a "second echelon" or weekend area. Typically a two- to six-hour drive on Friday night, the weekend area offers nearby lodging, 1,500 or 2,000 feet of vertical plunge, excellent snow grooming, an active social scene, and an efficient ski school. The Poconos, Catskills, Berkshires and New Hampshire lake district are full of such places, and you'll find them in northern Michigan, Quebec and throughout the Northwest. The pace is frenetic at most weekend resorts, largely because this is a stopping-off place for families, and skiers with ambition—suburban teenagers training to race, college kids yearning to be full-time ski bums, city singles pushing back the limits of a bar-scene social life.

A ski resort that does most of its business on weekends has much of the atmosphere of an ocean-side resort. Couples with kids own second homes there, or rent condos for the season. City singles bunk together in "share" households.

"During the winter, we live to ski," says Bill Spitz, a New York businessman in his late thirties. "For fifteen years, my friends and I drove six hours every Friday night, arriving in Sugarbush at midnight if we weren't stopped for speeding. It was crazy. Every year we rented a house together, basically the same group of people I hung out with in the summer.

It was a different house every year, but the routine was always the same: one person was responsible for cooking breakfast on Saturday, we skied together, we all went out to dinner Saturday night and partied at home until about one AM. Somebody else was responsible for breakfast Sunday morning, we skied together, and headed back to the city mid-afternoon. We had clean-up committees, and snow-clearing committees, and booze committees. We had romances, and protracted negotiations over privacy. We raced to use the shower on Saturday evening because there was never enough hot water, so couples showered together. We had rules about how many hair dryers could be run at once, because otherwise someone had to run to the basement to change the fuses. It was like boarding school, or summer camp."

Today, married to someone less enthusiastic about skiing, Bill won't drive twelve hours each weekend. Instead, he saves his money for a couple of big "destination" trips each winter.

A destination resort, almost by definition, is a place you have to fly to unless you are lucky enough to live in Denver or Salt Lake City or Reno. Above 6,000 feet lies paradise, a place so high that the snow clings deep and forever despite a bright, warm sun, where tanned snowgods wheel down 3,000-foot verticals, where a hotel stay lasts a week and you don't use your car, where you'll take a ski lesson just to learn how to deal with snow so good you can't stand it. In good weather, the big resorts of Northern New England and Quebec qualify as destination places: Colorado, Utah, Idaho, Wyoming, New Mexico and the Sierra resorts of California and Nevada are prime. Before going to these altitudes, city skiers learn to breathe the thin air by running,

Stowe, Vermont, is the East's largest destination ski resort. *(Stowe/Brownell)*

Sun Valley, Idaho, one of the best known destination ski resorts in the West. *(Bob Jonas)*

cycling, and dancing aerobically.

Destination resorts draw skiers who can afford fantasy mountain homes and families, singles and clubs on a once-a-year fling. They also draw people who live to ski, at any price—ski bums who would rather wait tables or tend bar at night and ski all day than pursue careers in the city. Mountain towns like Stowe, Aspen, Ketchum, and Truckee are populated largely by dropouts from city life. Their businesses provide most of the local services. They tend to outnumber native locals by a fair margin. A town like Vail didn't even exist twenty-five years ago. In essence, there are no natives.

Who are these dropouts? One such person is Tom Lippert. He was an elementary school teacher who came truly alive, by skiing, only two days a week at Squaw Valley. In 1975, after a decade of grading arithmetic tests, he said the hell with it, and bought a ramshackle house in Truckee for less than $10,000. He went to work at Squaw, teaching skiing full time, supplementing his income by scraping together a small photography business.

Today the photography business is a precarious full-time living, but Tom is satisfied. "Who needs a paycheck?" he asks. The ramshackle house has been lovingly converted into a ramshackle studio, and Tom still teaches skiing occasionally at Squaw, although the photo business provides more than enough travel and adventure to keep life bubbling. Magazines and advertising agencies send him flying around the world to ski and take pictures, in Europe, South America, throughout North America. His wife, Laurel, a writer, often travels with him. "It felt like I was taking a big risk when I moved here, but this is how I needed to live," Tom says. "I'd have gotten sick if I'd stayed in the city."

WHO SKIS?

All kinds of people ski, but on average skiers are a varied and interesting lot. Roughly eight million people ski regularly—more than ten days a year—in the United States. The cold statistics, according to *Ski* magazine research, say that these folks are well heeled: Average age, mid-thirties. Average household in-

Skiers are of all ages and inclinations. Clockwise from above: Senior citizens enjoy a day of cross-country track skiing. *(John Plummer)* Tots race on a cross-country track. *(John Plummer)* Backcountry hut skiers. *(Bob Jonas)* Practicing Alpine race technique. *(Sun Valley Trekking/Brettnacher)*

come, over $58,000. Average education, completed college. But averages don't tell us much about real, individual people or the thousands of families nationwide who can hardly wait for winter and skiing. There are the fascinating folks who live at the ends of the bell curve. The ski bum, for instance, who skis over ninety days a year, scrapes by on tips and hourly wages. The wealthy businessman, with a three-million-dollar vacation home in Vail, may ski thirty days a year and declare a stratospheric personal income. A retired dentist, who built a cabin near Lake Tahoe twenty years ago, may now ski all winter long on a comfortable retirement income. That skiers come in too many different shapes and lifestyles to characterize is one of the joys of the sport: skiers are constantly singling up on chairlifts with people who live uniquely interesting lives.

SKIING IN EUROPE

In Europe, where population centers are closer to the big mountains, people make fewer sacrifices to ski. Austrians and Swiss, not to mention Norwegians, Swedes and Finns, regard skiing as a backlot sport the way we Americans regard baseball. It's something school-children do daily. The same is true in parts of France, Italy and Germany, though a Parisian counterpart of Bill Spitz will, like him, drive long distances every weekend to ski. Because it's practiced universally, skiing is a more democratic sport in Europe. A larger proportion of the nation's children, well heeled or not, are introduced to skiing early, in school. Central Europeans also have access to the astounding Alps, rising (in France) to over 15,000 feet. A typical ma-

jor European resort may string together ninety lifts, crossing whole mountain ranges from village to village, province to province, even nation to nation—there are plenty of places where skiers can ride lifts to cross from France to Italy or Switzerland, from Italy to Austria or Switzerland, without benefit of clearing customs. And the terrain is equally astonishing: a descent of 6,000 vertical feet is not uncommon, though 3,000 feet is typical.

The western Alps of France and Switzerland are the highest mountains in Europe. In February—a month of school holidays in France—the ski stations fill up with vacationing families. Rooms are not to be had, and Americans who ski in Europe learned long ago to avoid February. Most French resorts are ultra-modern, super-efficient lift-and-lodging complexes built high above the foggy valley villages on sunlit mountain shoulders. The exceptions are the resorts established before the war: Chamonix and Val d'Isere, where everything still centers on the original village.

In Austria, most ski areas grew upward from existing towns, as local farmers installed lifts and built hotels. The country has literally hundreds of local lift networks, linked together over ridgelines to form chains of villages. Only a few of the grander complexes have achieved international attention, notably St. Anton, Innsbruck and Kitzbühel. But an intrepid skier with a smattering of German could spend a whole winter exploring the glacial valleys and ranges of Tyrol and Pongau, riding only lifts and trolley cars.

Switzerland, that independent amalgam of all that is best of Gallic, Teutonic and Latin cultures, combines French-style and Austrian-style resorts. Older towns—St. Moritz, Zermatt, Murren—

are villages. Newer ones, like Verbier and Les Diablerets, are French-style stations.

In Scandinavia and the snowier parts of Russia, of course, children have to ski just to get to school. In these lands, literally millions of people ski, and they ski daily, during the one-hundred-eighty-odd days of winter. There are relatively few lifts; cross-country is the primary ski sport.

In Japan skiing is not a form of daily transportation, but half the population skis for fun. In a country the size of Japan this makes for sizable crowds on ski slopes, as five million skiers jostle for room to turn on any given weekend. The answer to the question of "Who skis?" is "Practically everyone."

It's hard to escape the fact that skiing is big business today. America's 650-plus ski resorts employ over 50,000 people full-time during the winter—and that counts only the people who work on the mountain. Another 100,000 or so work in ski resort hotels and restaurants, some 50,000 in the nation's 8,000 ski shops, and an inestimable number provide transportation, construction, catering, real-estate, medical, legal and other necessary services to the business. The retail trade in ski equipment and clothing amounts to a billion dollars in the United States each year; in Colorado alone, ski tourism brings in over a billion dollars each season. Worldwide, skiers purchase about five million pairs of skis each year, manufactured in France, Italy, Austria, Germany, Switzerland, Yugoslavia, Spain, Japan, the United States, Canada, Norway, Sweden and Finland. That doesn't include Eastern bloc production: most cross-country skiers in those nations use skis made in East Germany, Czecho-

slovakia and Russia. Counting Russia, the world population of frequent skiers may top thirty million.

Typical ski resorts the world over have to deal with an overabundance of customers on weekends, and a shortage thereof on weekdays. At many resorts, weekend skiers often have to wait forty minutes to climb on a ski lift; Mammoth Mountain, the closest big ski area to Los Angeles, is used to handling crowds of 20,000 Southern Californians each weekend. However, if you can get away to ski on a weekday, you may have the mountain all to yourself. All of this is reversed at the big destination resorts where people come once a year, traveling to and from the resort on the weekend. Locals ski hard on Sunday, when visitors are checking out of their rooms.

Skiers are independent people. No one goes skiing in order to stand in long lines. That's why a skier like Bill Spitz heads for the destination resorts when he can. It's why a dropout like Tom Lippert moves to a mountain town. It's why a native son like Bob Jonas turns from the lift-served mountain to hide out in the backcountry.

In recent years, many skiers have taken up cross-country skiing as an escape from lift lines. They simply take a break from the lifts whenever it gets crowded. To serve these cross-country skiers, most major ski areas have developed touring centers, often on a snow-covered golf course. The local ski shops and rental shops provide cross-country equipment as well as downhill gear, and there's cross-country instruction and guide service available too. Royal Gorge in California, Telemark Lodge in Wisconsin and the Trapp Family Lodge in Vermont are among the better known cross-country resorts. These places have

Royal Gorge cross-country resort. A major cross-country ski area, like California's Royal Gorge, offers extensive base lodge facilities as well as a large network of groomed trails. *(Tom Lippert)*

no lifts at all. Instead, they offer a wide variety of carefully maintained trails for beginners, intermediates and expert cross-country skiers, with fine lodges and first class instruction.

3
The White World

Snow, like skiing itself, is of infinite variety. Any skier can spend a lifetime simply learning about snow, and still meet with surprises daily. One late winter morning in Idaho's Sawtooth range, we started off on the 10,000-foot ridgeline next to Monolith Peak, a sheer rock outcrop. Here we plunged through hundreds of yards of creamy fresh snow, three feet deep. Our skis sank in the fluff; it boiled up over our chests. Lower down, the powder grew thicker, and our skis rode on a firm, windpacked surface. Descending to the valley, we crossed a stretch where yesterday's tracked-out slush had frozen overnight into something resembling broken concrete. On the lower east-facing slopes, which had been getting sunshine for a couple of hours, the night's frozen crust was corning up nicely, but at the bottom it was already slush.

That 4,000-foot descent took less than ten minutes of easy skiing, but it brought us through half a dozen kinds of snow, each offering a different texture and experience. This is typical of a big-mountain run. Part of the magic of skiing lies in the stirring beauty of winter. But its unending interest comes from the protean nature of the snow itself. The Total Skier learns to enjoy all forms of snow, on all kinds of terrain.

An Eskimo dictionary compiled 120 years ago by the missionary Friedrich Erdman identifies thirty-five different words for forms of snow and ice. *Keratanek* means crusted snow; *ijarovaujak* signifies shining crystals on the surface; *pukak* refers to dry saltlike snow, while *sakketok* is fresh loose snow fallen in a dead calm. *Kimukvuk* is snow unevenly drifed by a storm. *Akkilokak* and *maujak* are forms of soft snow; wet snow is called *machakak*. *Tinginek* is water ice scoured free of snow by the wind.

This taxonomy may seem to cover all possibilities, but there are many more types of snow Eskimos have never seen. Because the Eskimo makes his living largely from the sea and by following the great herds of caribou, he rarely climbs far above sea level. Yet in the thin, dry air of the mountain peaks, there is snow that attains a feathery evanescence impossible in the dense, moist sea-level air, however cold. Meteorologists identify ten major different types of airborne snow crystals, as well as hundreds of subtypes—and each type begins to change into new shapes as soon as it reaches the ground. Because of snow's infinite grades and textures, and because of its constantly changing nature, scientists are at a loss to describe snow's mechanical properties from moment to moment. They simply call it the most plastic of materials.

Skiers are fascinated by that plasticity. The ever-changing snow engenders different ways to ski, and different attitudes about skiing. New, light snow—powder—is a dream for the Alpine skier. It's airy and billows up around you as you ski. Skiing powder is the closest thing to effortless weightlessness. Many Alpine skiers follow the powder from slope to slope, mountain to mountain, country to country, devotedly. But powder, to the cross-country skier, may mean a slow track and lots of sweat.

At the other end of the texture scale is hard-packed snow—or ice. On ice the Alpine skier must be tenacious, levering sharp edges carefully and powerfully into the snow. Ice means the track skier flies over flat sections, descending hills cautiously. Many skiers won't go out when the surface of the snow has turned to ice—it can be that intimidating. Between these extremes the snow surface presents an infinite range of challenges and sensations.

If skiers learn to love the many natures of snow, they become hooked, to begin with, by snow's simple beauty. Snow is, first of all, the very symbol of purity. In prescientific cultures, snow is often associated with winter's death and spring's renewal—many mythologies explain winter as a god's or goddess's temporary departure to the underworld.

The average American city gets 28 inches of snow. Averages are tricky numbers. That 28 inches is arrived at partly by balancing the Sunbelt's zero inches with the 60-inch snowfalls in cities like Denver and Buffalo. In the high Rockies and Sierra, snowfall may average 400 to 1,000 inches in a winter. That is simply a function of physics: as air rises, its pressure and temperature drop. When the

temperature drops low enough for water vapor to condense—at 100 percent humidity—we get precipitation: rain if it's warm, snow if it's cold. Higher mountains force the air to high, cold elevations. We get more snow.

The rule of thumb is that snowfall at modest elevations is one-tenth as dense as water. That means 28 inches of snow equals 2.8 inches of rain. But unlike rain, snow stays where it falls, insulating the soil and fragile plants against the worst of winter's hard freeze. Snow is a good insulator, precisely because new snow is nine-tenths air. That's also why new snow is fluffy and light, why it flies in our faces when we ski in it.

Once snow is on the ground, it changes gradually. If the weather is sunny and dry, snow can "evaporate" quickly even at below-freezing temperatures, turning directly to water vapor and riding off on the breeze. This process is called sublimation.

If it all stays in place, snow may settle into a denser pack, about half water and half air, with neighboring grains of snow fusing to one another to make a firm, stable snowpack (snowpack simply means the entire quantity of snow resting on the ground). This process is called equitemperature metamorphism. Continued long enough, over several seasons, it causes the snowpack eventually to compact down into pure water ice—like the kind that floats in scotch.

There's another way snow can change, or metamorphose. When the air is very cold, snow near the warmer ground may sublimate then refreeze in fragile crystals called depth hoar or sugar snow. Because depth hoar is loose and unconnected, it forms a layer of weakness in the snowpack. This "hollow" layer may collapse under the weight of a skier atop the overlying snowpack, perhaps causing the skier to break through the surface up to the waist. On steep mountainsides, layers of weakness in the snow mean avalanche danger. Because depth hoar appears when the difference between the ground temperature and air temperature is large, this process is called temperature gradient metamorphism. It's a serious warning sign—backcountry skiers pay special attention to avalanche potential when they know depth hoar is present—and they're always looking for depth hoar.

A fourth type of metamorphosis—the melt-freeze cycle—changes the texture of snow at the surface. Warm air and sun melt the sharp lacy points off the snow crystals, reducing them to tiny round grains. At night, these grains refreeze, often sticking to one another so that over a period of several days—through several thaw and refreeze cycles—the grains grow into the larger pellets skiers call corn snow. Melt-freeze takes place mostly in warmer spring weather.

Other changes can take place at the surface. In cold clear midwinter weather, the surface frosts. Repeated frosts result in the growth of extraordinarily beautiful crystals called surface hoar, as fragile as depth hoar. Buried under a new fall of fresh snow, a layer of surface hoar becomes another layer of weakness that can produce avalanches immediately—or weeks later.

Ice crystals begin to form in the air whenever the air is below freezing. At "standard" temperature and atmospheric pressure (corresponding to about 50 degrees Fahrenheit at sea level) the air at 6,000 feet altitude is close to freezing. A light rain at 50 degrees in San Francisco can be a heavy snowfall in Donner Pass,

Surface hoar forms on the snowpack following prolonged periods of cold, dry weather. *(Bob Jonas)*

7,000 feet up; when it's warm and dry in New York or Boston, the weather may be 20 degrees and snowing 300 miles north and 2,500 feet up in the Green Mountains.

In North America, we enjoy prevailing winds from the southwest—often from the northwest in winter. This means that winter storms originating in mid-Pacific come ashore over the West Coast. As the moist air is pushed upward over the Sierra and Cascades, it cools, reaches dew-point, and drops its first load of snow, generally on land lying from 3,000 feet to the highest West Coast peaks, over 10,000 feet. East of the Coast ranges is desert and plateau, broken by a few smaller ranges, which get their share of snow. But the next major obstacles, forcing the wind from the 5,000-foot desert floor up over 10,000 feet, are Utah's Wasatch and Idaho's Sawtooth ranges. The snow falling here, at interior elevations, is colder and drier than West Coast snow. In Colorado and Wyoming, storm-clouds encounter higher peaks still, releasing more snow.

The vast steppes of the Great Plains offer no impediment to blizzards sweeping down from the northwest, out of Canada. By contrast, the regular Pacific storm systems seem tame. Relieved of most of their moisture, the Pacific systems gather new strength in the flight across the flatland, reinforced by cold arctic air rushing in behind them from the Canadian north. They pick up some water over the Great Lakes, dump huge wet loads of snow on the eastern shores of those lakes, and deposit the rest in the Adirondacks and New England. There, where the mountains rise 3,000 to 5,000 feet, the storms leave dense, moist snow that quickly consolidates to ice.

That's the classic pattern. In a good snow year, storms line up in the Pacific and come ashore every four or five days. In some years the jet stream—a steady 100 mph wind above 30,000 feet—is "blocked" by a high pressure ridge in the Pacific, and swings far north to Alaska instead of coming ashore in California and the Northwest. From Alaska the blocked storm track swings south through the Midwest, missing the mountains. In those years southerly breezes bring warm weather and relatively poor snow to the West, while arctic air following the jet stream hammers the East with long periods of subfreezing weather. But even in these unusual years, natural snowfall in the Sierra and Rockies, at 8,000 to 14,000 feet, is deeper than in the 5,000-foot ranges of the East.

Because the snow is different depending on where, and how high, the mountains intercept the storms, the skiing itself varies tremendously from one mountain range to another. The finest, lightest powder is to be found at the highest elevations—and the snow is drier and lighter yet if those mountains, like Utah's Wasatch, lie downwind from a desert. High mountains downwind from

the ocean, like the Sierra and Cascade ranges, get moist snow—"Sierra cement"—in huge quantity. Low mountains like the Adirondacks get less snow, with a relatively high moisture content.

Because most skiers have access only to mountains near convenient transportation, we are used to temperate-zone ranges: the Alps, Appalachians, Rockies and Sierra in the Northern Hemisphere, the Southern Alps of New Zealand and Andes in the Southern Hemisphere. We don't usually think about skiing the perennially snow-cloaked mountains of the Arctic and Antarctic. But even temperate zone mountains offer an astounding variety of snow conditions. In the high mountain ski areas, new snow most often arrives as *powder*—cold and dry at high elevations, and so light that in Colorado locals may call it "champagne" or "cold smoke." When it's this light, you can gather it into a mitt and then blow it all away with less effort than it takes to extinguish a birthday candle. Compressed underfoot, dry powder contains so little lubricating moisture that it squeaks. It drifts in the trees and gullies into bottomless depths—we ski it weightlessly, floatingly. Rolled flat by grooming machines, light powder makes into Vail's vaunted "ego snow," so easy to ski that beginners quickly find themselves looping long 20 mph turns. In Utah and Colorado local skiers take powder for granted, and often decline to ski in anything else.

At lower elevations powder falls thicker, in a creamy sweet consistency that skis like whipped cream, or, after a nasty Pacific blizzard, like butter, sucking and trapping skis. This is classic Sierra cement. In California and the Pacific Northwest, skiers say if you can ski the cement, you can ski anything. Groomed,

Skiing "champagne" powder in the high mountains of Colorado. *(Vail/Vig)*

it settles down into a solid, impenetrable base, ideal race-course conditions—a smooth, edgeable carpet that will stand up to spring rain and last well into the summer.

Where dry new snow is exposed to strong, steady wind it packs down into *windslab,* a dry, inconsistently firm surface that may or may not support a skier's weight. Where it's smooth and thick, the windslab makes exhilarating skiing, but where it breaks it's treacherous. You find windslab on the windward sides of high, exposed peaks, and on the flanks, where wind funnels around a corner or through a saddle (the low ridge stretched between neighboring peaks). Look for windslab

on the top of an old powder deposit after a major wind shift has brought the storm in from a new direction. Sometimes the windslab is rippled, like the sand on the bottom of a lake. Sometimes it's carved into weird aerodynamic wavelike ridges or *sastrugi,* and thus frozen into nearly unskiable form.

In addition to wind, the snow surface is affected by temperature and sun. Early in the winter, when days are short and temperatures cold, surface snow may lie undisturbed and unchanged for several days; snow texture on all slopes tends to be uniform. But later, as temperatures rise above freezing on sun-struck slopes, surface snow changes rapidly; eastern and northern slopes, sheltered from the midday and late-afternoon sun, have radically different snow than you'll find on south- and west-facing slopes.

Undisturbed, a fresh fall of powder is transformed, after a day or two of bright sunshine, into *suncrust.* Suncrust begins on south- and west-facing exposures, and spreads, in warmer weather, to eastern faces. Thick suncrust will support a skier's weight, but if you break through, it will trap your skis under its armor plate. Sometimes you can lift pieces of suncrust from the surface an inch thick and up to a yard in diameter. More often it breaks up into chunks the size of dinner plates. Where it's breakable, the crust is very difficult to ski. Where unbreakable, it's as easy to ski as any firm, edgeable surface.

Several sunny days, separated by freezing nights, turns a smooth undisturbed surface into *corn snow.* The cycle of melting, refreezing and melting breaks the surface into clusters of icy granules, into which the ski edge slips effortlessly. Corn snow is fast, easy and

Wind and cold may shape snow into wavelike ridges called sastrugi, common to the high backcountry, but rarely experienced by the lift-served skier. *(Bob Jonas)*

delightful to ski, the spring treat experienced skiers await eagerly in late March and April. Local skiers go to the backcountry into May and June, just to ski the corn.

At higher elevations, very cold weather can suck the moisture out of dense, wet powder, drying it into finer, lighter snow. At lower levels, cold wind tends to pack the snow into a dense, settled pack. The ultimate result of snow settling is a firm, tough surface. Throughout the country, when confronted with snow so firm that an edge won't set easily, skiers complain about icy conditions. But only in the Midwest and East can skiers confidently claim to ski on *ice*. Ice, they say in New England, is what

you put into your drink. It ain't ice unless you can see through it, down to the underlying grass and rocks, down to last winter's old lift tickets. Pure water ice can be boilerplate hard, bulletproof hard. Like Californians, Vermonters say if you can ski their own chosen snow, you can ski anything. The worst case is snow, followed by rain, followed by a hard freeze. In the Sierra, the Midwest and New England alike, that cycle produces a thick, slick hide of ice on trees, powerlines and ski slopes. It glitters, but it isn't gold.

Beyond these naturally occurring snow conditions, lift-served skiers deal daily with surfaces created by traffic—that is, by other skiers and snowcats. An hour after the lifts open, a fresh fall of powder has been crisscrossed and churned into cut-up *junk snow,* inconsistent in texture and tricky to ski. Depending on whether it started out light or dense, junk snow may feel like meringue, mashed potatoes or extra chunky peanut butter. Several hours later, the passage of more skiers will pack it down into a consistent firm surface.

Snowcats often roll junk snow smooth before the skiers can. If the snow becomes too firm, the cats abrade the surface with a tiller sled, making it easier to edge on the slope. Snowcats are also equipped with bulldozer blades to flatten out moguls, those irregular hard bumps in the snow caused by many skiers turning at the same places on a slope.

At many cross-country centers the snow is groomed as intensely as at any lift-served mountain. Track skiers won't even venture out into fresh snow—not until the machines have smoothed the entire course and set precise, firm-walled tracks. The track skier never deals with junk snow—as soon as the track walls begin to break down, or the skating lane becomes rutted, the snowcat makes it all silken again.

It's the backcountry skier who comes to know most about the dynamics of snow. In the backcountry, a skier must be aware not only of surface texture, but of layers deep within the snowpack—layers of strength, layers of stress, potential weakness. When you deal with snow that may avalanche, what you don't know can kill you, suddenly. So the backcountry skier learns the snowpack from the ground up. And he skis snow never experienced by groomed-snow skiers: sastrugi piled up in frozen waves, jumbled avalanche deposition frozen hard like jagged bowling balls, tall powder hedges windrowed between the trees, the ice of

frozen lakes, the rimed pads of gurgling snow covered streams, the giant corn of good glacier ice, the feathery surface hoar tinkling like flimsy plastic Christmas decorations under his skis.

Just as we ski hundreds of different kinds of snow, we ski mountains in myriad shapes and sizes. Mountains grow and change according to long cycles and are every bit as plastic as the snow itself. Mountains are built by movements in the earth's crust. Continents float like rafts on the earth's fluid magma; as they jostle and bump, like huge lily pads, they buckle and fold at the edges into big young mountain ranges, like the Alps, Sierra and Rockies, which are still rising.

Alpine skiers break up islands of junk snow before a snowcat rollers it smooth. *(Sun Valley Co.)*

Backcountry skiers ascend the icy nose of a glacier in Alaska. *(Bob Jonas)*

Then the weather begins its work, grinding and polishing the mountains down smooth again. Through glacial action, thermal cracking, rain and the erosion of spring runoff, the greatest mountains are carried down to the plains, deltas and seas. Older mountains, like the Appalachians and Adirondacks, are therefore smoother, lower, more rounded.

Ski runs are also shaped by trees. In the East, hardwood forests climb all the way to the summits of our ski hills, and we can ski only because the trees were cut and hauled to build trails. This often means the trails are narrow, winding tracks through thick woods.

At the higher elevations of the Rockies and Sierra, only the hardier pines and aspens grow, and they grow more sparsely, thinning gradually as they rise to timberline, the point where the soil and weather will no longer support a tree. Above timberline the skiing is wide open—and even below timberline there are vast avalanche bowls and windy ridges that won't support forest. Some of the most delightful open skiing is on burns, old forest-fire sites.

When a lift-served ski mountain is developed, the ski runs are cut carefully through the woods. Ski area managers try to provide skiers a variety of challenging runs. Usually the timber on a mountain is removed in wide swaths, cleared to follow the natural fall line. Naturally open terrain is made accessible; runs are cut on all exposures, though north-facing slopes, which hold their snow longest, are a ski area's bread-and-butter.

Because there are many more skiers

of intermediate skills than there are experts, most lift-served ski areas try to provide more interesting, scenic fun trails—we could call them cruisers—than hair-raising steep runs. But any ski trail can be a challenge, especially when snow conditions change from smoothly groomed to difficult. Downhill skiers themselves create another terrain problem: moguls.

Moguls may be shaped like VW Beetles or sharks' teeth, depending on the steepness of the slope and the sharpness of the turns of the skiers who formed them. Good bumps are sized to match your skis, which slip between them naturally. Nasty bumps are sized to match someone else's skis, and can pound your knees to jelly or kink your back. But moguls are such an addiction for some skiers that they do nothing else but thread the bumps. They are as devoted to mogul terrain as powderhounds are to powder snow.

Because the snow and terrain are endlessly varied, lift-served skiing is endlessly challenging. When you've mastered the terrain on your home mountain, you can go to another mountain—nearby, or in a distant country. Because skiers travel the world, an international coding system has developed to warn them about the difficulty of trails they encounter—the signs serve as warnings to beginners not to tackle very difficult terrain, and as invitations to experts to add one more thrill to the diary, one more feather in the cap. The international code is simple: green signs identify easy trails, blue signs intermediate trails, red signs difficult trails and black signs top experts trails. In the United States, the system is simpler: green means easy, blue more difficult, black most difficult. To aid the color-blind, green signs are round, blue signs square, black signs diamond-shaped.

Cross-country trails are marked similarly. An easy trail follows very gradual and gentle hills, while a more difficult one includes some steep climbs and descents. The natural terrain dictates the direction a cross-country trail will take—while touring centers cut some trails through the woods, they are apt to route most trails through open country, following streams and valleys, bare southerly slopes and ridgelines, or old roadbeds. While lift-served downhill trails may be a few hundred yards to a mile-and-a-half long, cross-country trails are laid out in loops to provide five, ten and thirty kilo-

Two Alpine skiers negotiate a moguled slope. *(Sun Valley Co.)*

A backcountry skier telemarks between trees in new powder snow. *(Reid Dowdle)*

meter runs—three to eighteen miles of skiing.

Close to home, with no track nearby, the touring skier may blaze his own trail through wood lots and over rolling farmland. A favorite route may follow a fence line or skirt the edge of a wood, sheltered from the prevailing wind. In North America, most skiing is defined by the trees.

Much of the skiing in the Alps is far above timberline—there are ski areas in the high valleys of France where not a single tree stands in the lunar landscape. Colorado and Utah are more hospitable: there, even the highest ski areas have some trees struggling up the ridgelines. Expert skiers love the trees: the woods shelter the snow, breaking the wind to protect the powder. The day after a new snowfall, when the powder has been churned into moguls on the open slopes and trails, you may wonder where all the good skiers went.

They're hiding in the woods.

4
EQUIPMENT

Look at a ski. It's aesthetically perfect. It shares with the canoe, the flyrod and the sailplane a purposefulness of form that defies further simplification. We love each of these creatures first for the way it comes alive in its element, and then for its graceful, ineluctable organic shape.

For its unity, the ski is particularly appealing. It is a single family of related curves, with common origins and apices, forming a lively elliptical arch. That arch is a spring, a storer and restorer of kinetic energy, made to speed the skier from stride to stride or turn to turn. Around the midsection of the ski's running surface are grouped all its structural characteristics: the center of its arch (or camber), its narrowest point (or waist), the thickest part of its structure (the stiffest part of the spring), and its center of balance. Like the canoe and the flyrod, the ski is structurally and dynamically symmetrical in two axes.

The ski's symmetry and dynamism are not evident to the uninitiated, who see a simple plank with one end turned up. The first skis were just such simple planks, but 150 years of evolution and experimentation have led us to a ski that is a finely crafted tool, a friendly instrument to which a skier can dance with gravity.

Parts of a modern Alpine ski. *(Olin Ski Co.)*

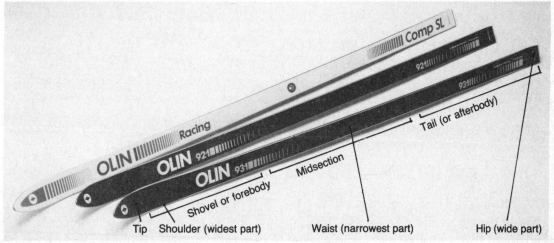

Tip Shoulder (widest part) Shovel or forebody Midsection Waist (narrowest part) Tail (or afterbody) Hip (wide part)

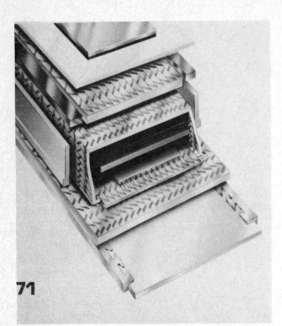

71

Exploded drawing of a typical modern slalom ski shows its foam core, multiple layers of fiberglass reinforcement (including a torsion box or wrap layer), steel edges and polyethylene base, and protective plastic sidewalls, topskin and top edges. *(Rossignol Ski Company)*

Look now at a typical cross-country track ski. Light and springy, it rests on the snow at tip and tail—toe and heel. Its long, strong center arches clear of the snow's surface. If you put two skis side-by-side and stand on them both, half your weight goes on each ski. The skis will compress under your weight, but since they share the work, each ski is only partially flattened: there is still a little air between the snow and the center of the ski. The soft-flexing tip and tail have flattened completely, of course; you can push with poles and glide easily on the hard, smooth surfaces at the front and back of the skis.

We put a "kicker" on the running surface of the arch, that short center sec-

tion still held clear of the snow. Skiers often call this the wax pocket. The kicker may be a layer of soft sticky wax, or a section of base with a machined pattern or chemical treatment that resists sliding backward. If you now step firmly down and back on one ski, all your weight and strength engage to flatten out the camber and press the kicker into the snow. The kicker grips the snow, and you thrust against it, striding the opposite ski into a long, easy glide. The kick finished, your kicking ski rebounds into its own glide; for a moment you are suspended, sliding easily on equally weighted skis, kicker arches clear of the snow. When you kick down and back on the other ski, an elegantly simple cycle repeats. Kick and glide, kick and glide, kick and glide.

To help achieve a long, efficient kick and glide on smooth, manicured tracks, cross-country ski boots have evolved into light, flexible shoes, very close in feel to good running shoes. There are important differences: a cross-country track shoe obviously has to lock into a toe binding of some sort, and in order to help you balance on the light, narrow ski, the ski boot sole is machined to mate with a binding connection that is rigid laterally and torsionally; the boot sole itself has to

A cross-country track ski has a raised midsection providing a "wax pocket." When the skier places all his weight on the ski, it flattens, distributing the weight into the tail and shovel during the glide phase, or compressing the wax pocket into the snow for grip during the push-off or kick phase of cross-country track striding.

A cross-country track shoe mates to a specific toe binding. The boot/binding "system" may vary among manufacturers.

resist twisting. So cross-country shoes today are built with very springy nylon soles, which won't flex sideways while they bend very easily up and forward into a stride.

Naturally, the flex or springiness of your cross-country skis must be matched accurately to your weight and ability: if you have a very strong kick, you'll flatten a soft-flexing kicker prematurely and that will restrict your glide; you'll be dragging your wax pocket around on the snow all the time, feeling hobbled. If your skis are too stiff for you, the kicker will never engage; each time you kick back, the ski will slide backward. You'll make no progress, and climbing hills is out of the question. So your most critical decision, in choosing a cross-country track ski, is to find the right flex pattern. Rely on the advice of an experienced ski instructor or cross-country ski shop; it takes many miles of kicking and gliding on many different skis to develop a feel for softer and stiffer models. The "paper test" is a useful guide: on a smooth firm floor, step on a ski. Its camber should flatten, lightly pinning a single sheet of paper laid under it. A friend should be

able to withdraw the paper with a firm, smooth tug.

The other critical decision in choosing a cross-country ski regards width. Wider skis are easy to balance on, and float across smooth unbroken snow more easily, but are heavy and glide less effectively on tracks. Narrow skis glide like the wind on groomed tracks, but off the track bog and sink in ungroomed snow. Choose a ski appropriate to where you'll ski most often: for in-track skiing, pick a relatively narrow *light touring ski* about 50 mm wide, and as you improve change to an even lighter, narrower *racing ski* about 45 mm wide.

If you want to skate around track trails, you can use a racing ski, or choose a specialized *skating ski*—about 10 cm shorter than a traditional racing ski, with lower camber and stiffer flex to resist the powerful skating thrust. If you plan to ski off prepared tracks—at a local golf course or forest preserve with ungroomed snow—get a slightly wider *touring ski* about 55 mm wide. Later, when you take up backcountry skiing, you may want a heavy-duty steel-edged *cross-country/downhill ski* 60 mm wide, or even wider. It's common for good cross-country skiers to own a pair each of racing skis, touring skis and cross-country/downhill skis, and to choose the pair appropriate for the day's snow conditions and planned itinerary. If you can afford just one pair of skis, you'll find the touring ski most versatile. It won't be light and nimble on the track, but it will work there, and it won't allow you to descend steep terrain in difficult snow, but it will let you learn to descend gentle slopes safely.

Choose your cross-country boots to match your skis. A light, narrow racing or light touring ski works well with a

TYPES OF CROSS-COUNTRY SKIS

Type	Width	Boot to use	Purpose
Racing	45 mm	Racing	Racing, training in track. Available waxable or waxless, or in special version for skating.
Light touring	50 mm	Light touring	Learning, training, skiing in track. Available waxable or waxless.
Touring	55 mm	Touring	Learning, training, skiing off track. Available waxable or waxless.
Steel-edge XC downhill	60 mm	Telemark or double boot	Backcountry, telemark, mountaineering. Normally waxable; use climbing skins for steep ascents.

CROSS-COUNTRY SKIS: WAXABLE OR WAXLESS

Today, most new cross-country skiers start off on waxless skis. Waxless skis, which provide a textured kicker pattern on the ski base to help prevent the ski from sliding backward, work the same way traditional waxable skis work—the kicker pattern simply takes the place of the soft kicker wax, which must be applied to the central wax pocket on a waxable ski.

Experienced skiers still generally prefer the glide characteristics of waxable skis, and as you improve in technique the time will come when you should try a waxable ski, and learn how to wax it properly. Waxable skis are most often light touring or racing skis meant for fast skiing in tracks. A properly waxed ski is a joy, delivering optimum glide and consistent kick for the prevailing snow conditions. For information on how to wax cross-country skis properly, see pages 134–137 in Chapter 9.

High performance skiing is possible on a waxless ski—just wax the tip and tail with a glider wax for a long, fast glide, and let the kicker pattern function in place of the kick wax.

So: choose a waxless ski to keep things simple, or a waxable ski for ultimate high performance.

light, low-cut, flexible shoe mated to a light, integrated binding. Skate systems are stiffer than traditional striding systems so that the ski will be held close to the shoe sole when you lift it after the skate, instead of dipping back down on the snow (an advantage for striders who stay in the tracks). A wider touring ski, designed to go off track into deeper snow, requires a higher, warmer boot, with a slightly stiffer sole to control the heavier ski. The binding and boot are usually separate entities rather than an integrated system. For cross-country downhill and telemark skiing, use a tough leather over-the-ankle boot with a

A cross-country boot and binding for backcountry skiing is much heavier and more supportive than a cross track shoe/binding system. The 75 mm 3-pin binding mating to a boot with corresponding pin holes—shown in this drawing—is universal among manufacturers.

heavy-duty midsole and Vibram shoesole. This boot is, in effect, a mountaineering boot modified to work with a heavy-duty three-pin Nordic ski binding. It's designed to control a ski on very difficult terrain, and to keep feet warm and dry in cold, wet conditions. Look for integrated boot/binding systems in all three realms of cross-country in the future.

Because cross-country is a self-powered sport, cross-country skis and boots have grown progressively lighter over the years. After all, on every stride you must pick up your ski and boot and put them down again—the less weight you have to lift and kick, the easier, longer and smoother your stride may be. But light weight may not be consistent with the high speed stability and accurate edge control necessary for gravity-powered downhill skiing, so Alpine skis have grown gradually wider and, with the addition of metal layers, somewhat heavier. Today, the narrowest Alpine skis—the slalom racing skis used by many experts—are about 65 mm wide at the waist. A forgiving, easy-to-balance-on beginner ski will measure about 70 mm wide. Look closely at a downhill ski and you'll see a flatter, gentler arch. More important, the ski's sides curve deeply, from a wide tip to a narrow waist to a wide tail. This curve is called sidecut, and it forms the ski's steering edge. When a skier flexes his knees and ankles subtly to tilt the ski up on edge, the ski rides on that curve. Naturally, it turns.

Because a downhill ski has no wax pocket, but a single smooth line of camber from tip to tail, it flexes into a smooth single curve, often called the ski's natural turning radius. Some skis—longer racing skis, for instance—naturally carve long, sweeping turns; shorter, softer-flexing skis naturally carve shorter, easier turns. Lots of short turns help slow a skier down; long sweepers imply high speed. So beginners generally do better on shorter, more maneuverable skis.

A soft-flexing ski helps a beginner in another way. Because of its soft flex pattern, most of the skier's weight is concentrated on the snow directly underfoot, with little pressure transferred to the tip and tail. With the ski flat on the snow, the

Skis for the three worlds of skiing differ significantly. From top to bottom: an Alpine ski, a cross-country backcountry ski, and a track ski.

Ski's Golden Rule to Ski Length

Answer each question by checking the appropriate number, then add up your points to determine your recommended ski length in centimeters.

How much do you weigh?	Points
Over 200 lb.	52
180–200 lb.	50
160–180 lb.	49
140–160 lb.	48
120–140 lb.	45
100–120 lb.	42
80–100 lb.	40
60–80 lb.	35
Under 60 lb.	30

How do you ski?	
Smooth and stable	55
Fast through the bumps	50
Motoring quietly	42
Not always upright	35

How aggressively do you ski?	
Fast and fearless	50
Generally game	48
Getting better	45
Easygoing	43
Cautious	40
Terrified	35

Where do you ski?	
Gates and wide open spaces	50
All terrain	48
Mostly moguls	45
Purely packed powder	43
Easy stuff	40

Your total score:
Total points equals recommended ski length.

skier can, upon weighting the ski, swivel or steer it fairly easily.

Most people start skiing on short, wide rental skis. After you've skied a few days, consider buying your own equipment. One problem with skiing on rental gear is that every day you have to get used to the new boots and skis before you can begin learning anything. Your own skis and boots will be known quantities—

there will be no adjustment period early every morning. Even more important, they will fit you properly, and for that reason, will be easier to control.

Choosing the correct ski length can be a confusing process. Here's a ski-length selector chart developed by *Ski* magazine, which works well for the vast majority of skiers:

Once you've found the right ski length, consider where you'll be skiing. If in the East or Midwest—largely on firm snow—look for a quick-turning fiberglass slalom-type ski. If in the West, on softer snow, you should be able to use a slightly wider, softer giant slalom-style ski, of fiberglass or aluminum.

If the Golden Rule says you should be using skis 200 cm or longer (190 cm or longer for women), look for a versatile racing ski. If your score says you should be using 185-200 cm skis (175–190 cm for women), look for a good "sport" or "performance" ski. And if your score falls under 185 cm (175 cm for women), look for a soft, wide, more forgiving "recreational" model.

Ski quality is largely a matter of materials, particularly of the plastic used for the base. All skis now use some grade of polyethylene, but cheap skis have bases of soft *extruded* polyethylene, while high-quality skis use a much harder, more durable *sintered* polyethylene. The sintered material resists damage much better, and glides faster and more smoothly. It's worth paying a few extra dollars for a ski with a bona fide sintered base. Unfortunately, you can't tell extruded from sintered bases just by looking, so you'll have to rely on the salesman's advice, on the manufacturers' literature, and on the reports in *Ski* magazine for information on each of the current models.

To control your downhill skis accu-

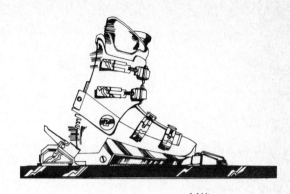

The modern Alpine boot and binding is far more rigid and supportive than cross-country boot/binding systems.

rately you'll need a pair of snug, close-fitting boots. Alpine ski boots are nothing like running shoes. They're like nothing used in any other sport. Alpine boots have evolved into rigid-soled plastic casts, able to transmit very small movements of the knee and ankle into equivalent movements of the ski edge. The boot is made in two parts: a stiff, dense, leakproof outer shell, usually molded of a polyurethane or nylon plastic, and a soft, insulating innerboot, to provide a warm cushion between the foot and the unyielding shell. If the innerboot is too soft and thick, the foot can move around inside the shell, with a consequent loss of control over the ski. In order to feel and control the ski, you need to find a boot shell that fits your foot accurately enough that the innerboot can be relatively thin and firm.

This is not to recommend that you buy an uncomfortable ski boot. If the boot is correctly designed and properly sized, it will be both warm and comfortable. A common mistake, made even by experienced skiers, is to select too large a boot, because it feels comfortable in the ski shop. Once the boot is latched into a

TYPES OF ALPINE SKIS

Type	Typical length		Typical width	Best use
	women	men		
Downhill	215-225 cm		72 mm	Downhill racing at over 50 mph
Super GS	205-215 cm		68 mm	Racing at 35-50 mph
Giant Slalom	200-210 cm		68 mm	Racing at 30-40 mph; expert skiing in soft snow
Slalom	190-205 cm		66 mm	Racing at 15 mph; skiing on firm snow or steep terrain
Recreational GS	190-205 cm		68 mm	Citizen racing, skiing in soft snow
Recreational slalom	190-205 cm		66 mm	Citizen racing, skiing in all snow
Soft long skis	185-205 cm		67 mm	Skiing in all snow
Mogul skis	190-205 cm		66 mm	Skiing in steep bumps
Powder skis	180-205 cm		69 mm	Skiing in deep snow
Sport skis	180-200 cm		67 mm	For intermediate to advanced skiers
Recreational skis	170-195 cm		67 mm	For beginner to intermediate skiers
Beginner skis	150-180 cm		68 mm	Beginners

ski binding, however, you have a great deal more leverage over it; suddenly you can feel your foot rolling around in there. In order to control your skis better, you'll buckle an oversized boot so tightly that you'll constrict the big veins that run down the top of your foot, and that leads almost immediately to cold toes and a miserable day on the mountain.

In fact, most skiers search years for the perfect ski boot, and it's wonderful to see what happens when a skier finally finds the boot that fits correctly. Overnight, his skiing may improve dramatically. He stands more naturally and comfortably on his skis, because the boots put him in just the right position. He can feel precisely what his skis are doing as they rise and fall over the terrain, as they flex and quiver underfoot (that sensation alone is one of the delights of the sport, as "road feel" is one of the delights of a sports car), because the boots transmit energy efficiently from ski to nerve endings. And he can control his skis with marvelously little effort, because the boots transmit energy equally efficiently in the other direction, from muscle to ski.

How can you short-circuit years of hunting for just the right ski boot, and go

Boots for the three worlds of skiing. Left to right: Alpine touring, Alpine downhill, cross-country track skiing, cross-country touring, and cross-country downhill. *(Bob Jonas)*

directly to a boot that fits your unique foot? The only way is to try on ski boots. Don't just try on three or four pairs in one shop, settling on the least uncomfortable. Instead, try on dozens of boots, in several ski shops if necessary. If possible, go to ski shows, where manufacturers bring in stocks of boots for people to try on. The more boots you try, the more you'll know about ski boots, and the closer you'll come to saying "Aha! True love at last!"

To speed you on your quest, here are some easy rules on what the perfectly fitting ski boot should feel like:

- The boot is comfortably snug. There are no uncomfortably tight spots or pressure points, and the toes have room to wiggle; forward flex is comfortable.
- The ball of the foot, the instep, heel and ankle are all so closely supported that they are immobile inside the boot.
- In particular, there is no uncomfortable chafing or pressure point on the shin or front of the ankle.
- When you do a knee bend, the boot flexes smoothly, with little or no bulging at the instep.

- When you do a knee bend, the heel of your foot doesn't rise off the insole of the boot.
- Fifteen minutes later, after you've hopped around vigorously in the boot, it's still comfortable and still snug.

Downhill bindings are also significantly heavier and more complex than cross-country bindings. Fortunately, they're easy to use. Modern bindings are almost universally step-ins. That means you can drop your skis on the snow, put your feet on the bindings and step down. The bindings close automatically, and you can ski off. When it's time to get out, you can lift a lever or press a button, usually with the tip of your ski pole, and the binding will release the heel of your boot. Walk away from your skis. It's about like getting into your car and buckling up the seat belt.

That's a pretty good analogy, because while the binding's prime function may appear to be holding your boots to your skis, the binding is really a safety device, just like the seat belt. Every skier falls down, and beginners more often. Sometimes we fall in such a way as to twist a leg. The binding is designed to release the boot from the ski before the leg is twisted or bent far enough to sustain injury. To prevent twisting, the toe unit allows the boot to rotate to either side, right and left. To prevent bending, the heel unit allows the boot heel to rise up away from the ski. The modern binding's spring-and-cam mechanism, protected inside its alloy or plastic housing, is programmed to sense torque on the boot and kick the boot loose when appropriate.

There are certain types of forces, of course, that no binding can protect against. Just as your seat belt won't save your life if a fast freight out of Denver crushes your car, a binding won't help much if you run into a tree, or dive off a cliff. It can't release the boot straight down through the ski, so if you land too hard off a jump you risk some kind of compressive injury. Having bindings that release, and which are kept in good, working condition, is every skier's responsibility, but just as seat belts don't confer the right to break traffic laws, bindings are no substitute for a healthy sense of self-preservation.

Select a ski binding according to your weight and ability; there's an industry-wide standard scale that assigns each skier a value corresponding very roughly to leg strength, and the binding you choose should cover your range on that scale. Called the DIN Scale (DIN stands for Deutsche Industrie Normen, or German Industrial Standards), the scale is used to calibrate all bindings. A good ski shop will help you determine your DIN number based on additional factors— sex, age, old injuries or propensity toward overweight, for instance—but most skiers can get a pretty good idea of their DIN scale setting from the chart below. Alpine ski poles are very simple. Made of aircraft-grade aluminum alloy tubing, they should reach the bottom of the rib cage: the rule of thumb is that when the poles are held naturally, with the tip of the pole in the snow, your forearm should be horizontal to the ground. Choose a grip and strap combination that feels comfortable in your gloved hand; as you progress, pole plant timing will become more and more important, and you should be able to swing your pole easily and naturally, without an awkward cock to the wrist. For this reason we recommend strongly that new skiers avoid strapless grips, which usually lock the wrist into a rigid position.

Poles for cross-country skiing are more complex. There are two kinds. For in-track skiing, choose a pole made of light, springy fiberglass or carbon fiber. Length is dependent upon whether you stride or skate. Traditional in-track striders use a pole just long enough to tuck under your armpits. Skating poles are 10 cm longer; they reach your lip. For backcountry skiing, stronger, stiffer aluminum is the safer material. Get a pair adjustable for length; you'll want a long pole for climbing and striding on the flat, and a shorter pole for skiing downhill.

Ski equipment is not cheap, and while skis, boots, bindings and poles should cost, altogether, less than a good set of golf clubs or a new sailboard, buying this stuff is not lightly undertaken. Once acquired, it should be properly, and regularly, maintained. Skis, to remain effective turning tools, must be flat-

DIN Standard Scale

DIN Number:	1	2	3	4	5	6	7	8	9	10
Beginner	40	60	90	110	130	150	170	190	210	230
Intermediate		50	80	100	120	140	160	180	200	220
Expert		40	70	90	110	130	150	170	190	210

(Body weight in pounds)

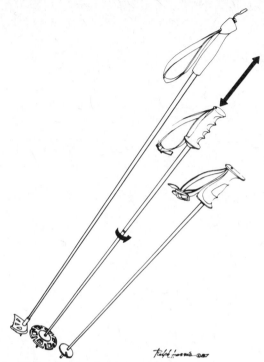

An Alpine and backcountry ski pole are much the same while the skating ski pole is significantly longer. Left to right: skating pole, adjustable backcountry pole and Alpine pole.

filed and waxed every couple of days (cross-country skis, of course, need to be cleaned and waxed daily). Ask an experienced friend, a ski instructor or ski shop mechanic, to teach you how this is done. It can be explained easily enough—it's a very simple procedure—but it requires a touch, the way finishing fine woodwork or baking good bread requires sensitivity to the materials. So it's best learned by watching real hands at work. There are now some good video tapes to learn this from, too. Boots should be kept clean and dry, bindings scrupulously clean, dry and lubricated. In particular, keep road salt off skis and bindings. Bindings should also be inspected and readjusted by a competent ski shop mechanic at least once a year, if only to adjust for boot sole wear.

A few words about used ski gear. You can often start cross-country skiing cheaply by shopping for well-maintained used equipment. Alpine gear is another story. For reasons explained above, used Alpine ski boots are a bad bargain. Used bindings are worse. Used skis can be excellent value if they've been properly maintained. If you know that a pair of used skis is appropriate for your skill level, and that it's just the right length for you, consider the condition of its bases and edges. The base should be smooth and waxed, the edges shiny and sharp, free of burrs and rust. Check the sidewalls for unevenness, which can be a sign that the skis have been repaired after a delamination. The conventional wisdom, for skiers on a budget, is this:

- Alpine skiers should spend whatever is necessary—and more, if that makes sense—to get the perfect ski boot. Ski boot fit is critical for the cross-country skier, too—and cross-country boots must also match the binding you plan to use.

The skating technique requires a longer pole than those needed for Alpine or backcountry skiing.

- With whatever cash you have left buy a pair of skis in the right length and flex pattern for the kind of skiing you do most; they don't have to be this year's model.
- Get good, new bindings; most ski shops will give you a discount on Alpine bindings or on a cross-country boot/binding system when you buy skis. They don't have to be top-of-the-line models, but they should be current. If you're going into the backcountry, make sure your bindings are equipped with runaway straps. You don't want to lose a ski in a place you can't walk out of. All good Alpine bindings come equipped with ski brakes, which will serve in place of runaway straps at any lift-served area.
- Save money by buying inexpensive Alpine poles, but cross-country poles should be of good quality—and never take cheap poles into the backcountry.
- Buy multipurpose clothing. By layering, you can arrive at a combination of clothing that will keep you warm, dry and comfortable regardless of the weather and regardless of the type of skiing you're doing that day. The inner layer should be of a knit polypropylene blend—polypro with wool or cotton—to keep moisture away from the body and keep a layer of dry air next to the skin. The next layer should be a fast-drying insulator, like polyester fleece. The third layer can, on bitterly cold days, be a down vest. The outer layer should be a windproof and waterproof shell. The initial cost of this system may be high, but because you can use it in its infinite variations for every type of skiing—and other cold-weather sports as well—it's a cost-effective purchase.

5
Fitness

Ironically, most skiers live near sea level. They commute each weekend from cities like Boston, New York, Seattle, San Francisco or Los Angeles to ski areas a mile or two high. There, if they haven't been exercising regularly, they flounder in the thin air, gasping for oxygen like landed fish. If you've ever felt your legs burning after your second run on Saturday morning, or felt weak and lightheaded before lunch, this chapter is for you.

There are three kinds of exercise critical to all skiers: aerobic exercise for improved heart and lung capacity, strength and power exercise for major muscle groups and flexibility exercise for smoothly functioning joints and muscles.

Aerobic conditioning is remarkably simple. Your heart is a muscle, and can be made stronger, like any other muscle, by exercising it. The goal is to build the heart up until it can move more blood, more quickly, through the lungs and out to overstressed muscles.

Obviously, it's dangerous to overtax the heart, so exercise to make it stronger should be approached conservatively. Most doctors and exercise physiologists now recommend basing your training on a "sub-max" concept. Sub-max refers to the minimum heartbeat rate that will produce a gain in heart strength. Here's how it works: First, calculate your sub-

max heart rate. It's easy. Subtract your age from 220; that figure is your approximate maximum safe heart rate. For a forty year old, the maximum rate is about 180 beats per minute, for a twenty year old, it's 200. These are numbers you should never exceed—maximum heart rate is your body's redline.

Now take 65 percent of your maximum heart rate. For a forty year old, that would be 117 beats per minute, for a twenty year old, 130 beats. This is your sub-max rate. As you exercise, the heart won't grow in strength unless you get your pulse up above the sub-max rate, and hold it there.

There are two more heart-rate figures to consider. The first is your anaerobic threshold, usually around 85 percent of your maximum heart rate— about 153 for a forty year old, 170 for a twenty year old. At the anaerobic threshold, the heart is functioning safely, but the skeletal muscles—the big muscles of the legs and torso that do the major work—are no longer getting enough oxygen. This is the point at which the muscles begin to fill with lactic acid— push the body beyond this threshold for more than a few minutes and you invite stiffness, soreness, even muscle injury. The threshold does vary, however. If you're not in training, it may be lower;

people in top-notch shape may be able to go to 90 percent of maximum heart rate for long periods of time without muscle distress. One of the goals of a training program is to raise the anaerobic threshold.

The final heart rate to consider is resting pulse—your normal pulse when you've been sitting around, reading or watching the tube, for the past half hour. Resting pulse can vary widely—in some highly trained athletes it may be around 40 beats per minute, while most healthy people have a resting pulse somewhere between 50 and 70. A resting pulse much higher than that may be some cause for concern. One of the ways to judge the success of a training program is to see if it lowers the resting pulse, and if it reduces the time necessary to restore a resting pulse after periods of heavy exercise.

A sensible aerobic training program starts with a target window: you want to bring your pulse up to some rate between sub-max and anaerobic threshold. For our conjectured forty year old in good general health, the target might be 75 percent of his maximum heart rate, or 135 beats per minute. The twenty year old could shoot for 150 beats.

If you haven't been exercising at all, begin carefully. On the first day, bring your pulse up to target gradually, after a warm-up period, and hold it there for ten minutes. Then cool off gradually. The form of exercise almost doesn't matter. It should be convenient, so you can do it daily, and fun, so you will do it daily. If you enjoy running, run. If you find running painful for feet and knees, or boring, bicycling might be a better choice. Swimming and rowing are both excellent, because they work out the upper body as well as the legs. Cross-training—swimming and bicycling on alternate days, for instance—is probably ideal, because it gives major muscle groups a forty-eight-hour rest between workouts, while giving the heart its daily exercise.

If you feel comfortable with the ten-minute workout, increase your target-pulse time to twenty minutes, then thirty minutes. At the forty-minute mark, you're beginning to do the heart and lungs some good. A one-hour workout is a good, solid time to shoot for. Maintain your target 75 percent pulse rate for one continuous hour each day, and you'll see rapid progress in physical condition. If you can only manage to get in your hour three or four times a week, it's still well worth doing.

Now a word of caution: if you have any history of heart problems, unusual blood pressure or weight problems, see your doctor before embarking on any exercise program.

Obviously, you'll have to learn how to take your own pulse, and monitor it while exercising, in order to reach and maintain your target rate. Find a pulse between the tendons on the inside of your wrist, or on either side of the windpipe just below your jaw. It's tough to take your pulse while jogging or swimming, and not safe to take one hand off the handlebars to do it while cycling. So plan to stop for fifteen seconds, long enough to get a quick count, then resume.

That gradual warm-up should never be forgotten. Never exercise cold, stiff muscles. Run in place, or do some gentle jumping jacks, until the blood starts moving easily through your legs, back and arms. Stretch each major muscle group, smoothly, without bouncing: rotate your head and neck, stretch the back and legs, flex the arms.

Heart Rate Chart

All figures approximate

Maximum pulse	210	200	190	180	170	160	150
Anaerobic threshold	178	170	161	153	144	136	127
Target pulse rate	157	150	142	135	127	120	112
Sub-max pulse	136	130	123	117	110	104	97
Age	10	20	30	40	50	60	70

Use the same warm-up routine before power training. Power training aims to develop strength in skeletal muscles. Running and cycling on hills are good power training for the legs, but skiing uses additional muscles for rotational and lateral power. Here are some good exercises for leg strength and flexibility, useful whether you plan to ski downhill, cross-country or backcountry:

EXERCISES

Quad power

Strong quadriceps are important for a powerful cross-country kick, for skiing moguls and gates on downhill skis, and for both climbing and telemarking on backcountry skis. Fortunately, most exercise devices provide at least one station for quad training. The basic routine is the leg press, in which the legs are used to push outward against resistance while you're seated. Leg lifts, done while lying face down or face up on a bench, and bending the knee against resistance at the ankle, are excellent exercises for quads and knees. Power sets are usually done in sets of ten repetitions. Build the kind of active strength you need for skiing by doing your repetitions quickly, at a comfortable weight. Do three sets of ten repetitions, then exercise another muscle group, and come back to the quad sets later.

If you don't have access to this kind of equipment, the best kind of exercise is to walk down stairs. At work and at home, make it a habit to ride the elevator up, but take the stairs down. To descend stairs works the same muscles you use braking and absorbing moguls on skis.

Lateral power

Many gyms have equipment that allows you to work the leg laterally—straight to the side. Nautilus exercise machines and Universal weight-training machines have stations to provide resistance as you lift the leg directly to the right or left. The exercise is important for skating power on the cross-country track and on the Alpine race course. This kind of strength can also be developed through an easy isometric exercise: just stand in a doorway and press your foot outward against the doorjamb. Press as hard as you can and hold it for fifteen seconds. Rest, then repeat. Over a period of time you can work up to one-minute presses.

Rotational power

Few exercise machines allow you to twist your foot, lower leg and knee against resistance, yet this kind of strength is the key to steering a ski—any kind of ski. But you have a resistance trainer for rotational strength in the closet: your own boots and skis. Put them on, then sit on a table or the edge of a porch—wherever you can extend your leg straight outward with the tail of the ski clearing the floor. With one leg extended, rotate the foot (and ski) smoothly to the left and right. Don't bounce the muscles—rotate the ski slowly and continuously as far as is comfortable, hold it there, then rotate back. Do five repetitions, then exercise the other leg. Repeat this, and work up gradually to twenty repetitions before resting the leg.

Sports that involve a lot of pivoting—singles tennis, soccer, and basketball, for instance—are also good for rotational power.

Arms and shoulders

Ambitious cross-country skiers need a strong poling technique. Rowing is a tremendous exercise for arms and shoulders, and so is the pulley-weight system found in most gyms. Universal and Nautilus machines have stations for a straight arm pull; use such a station in the same motion you'd use for poling, and also duplicate the double-poling motion.

SPECIFICITY TRAINING

Each type of skiing—Alpine, cross-country and backcountry—demands a different level of fitness. The recreational skier will find cross-country touring on gentle terrain the least demanding, with lift-served downhill skiing somewhat more taxing. Free-heel downhill takes more energy still, and fast cross-country track skiing is the most demanding of all. Racing-style cross-country skiing, in fact, is now recognized nationwide as the very best sport to develop complete fitness. Backcountry skiing requires all-around strength, too, but doesn't demand the continuous aerobic output of track skiing—you stop to rest frequently in the backcountry. It's not a competitive environment. However, backcountry skiing requires excellent leg strength and balance—you ski, carrying a pack, in mixed snow conditions.

The recreational Total Skier would do well to train for both Alpine downhill and cross-country track skiing—the combination will provide cross-over benefits in other types of skiing. Any training program should include all three types of exercises: endurance (aerobic), strength and flexibility. To achieve the maximum benefit, your conditioning program should be consistent from week to week and involve a systematic increase in training load. Rest and relaxation are very important, along with keeping well hydrated, and maintaining a diet that is 60 percent carbohydrates.

Given these general guidelines, it remains true that there is no training like skiing itself. For best results, exercises for skiing should simulate skiing. If you could ski every day of the year, you'd never have to get back into shape for skiing—but unless you travel to South America or New Zealand in the summer, you'll be off your skis at least six months each year. To train skiing muscles during the dry-land months, it helps to use ski-specific exercises.

Muscles are composed of fibers. Some fibers are used for strength, some for endurance, some for both. Different sports, and different modes of skiing, fire those fibers in specific, unique ways. It's the neuromuscular response to exercise at this motor unit level of muscle fibers that makes specificity training important. Running or cycling may keep your aerobic level high, but may not train the muscle fibers you need for skiing continuously. This is why cross-training is better than concentrating solely on aerobics, and why it's important that the summer exercise you choose should feel like skiing. For instance, the dry-land cross-country skier is better off on roller skis than on roller skates, and the Alpine skier can get more benefit from ski-step exercises using a Sport Cord exercise

Roller skiing is recognized as the best "dry-land" training technique for cross-country track skiing. *(John Plummer)*

Downhill running is an excellent training technique for downhill skiing. *(Bob Jonas)*

rope, or from ice skating, than from water skiing.

You may consider specificity training a form of fanaticism. It's true that rigid specificity training will yield big benefits for the active competitor—the Little League player, citizen racer or national team member. But the skier who devotes fifteen days a year or fewer to skiing will probably find specificity training downright boring, and won't do it.

Instead, spend the summer doing sports you enjoy enough to do regularly. Then, when the first colors of autumn blaze across the forests and the air turns crisp, you can think of specificity training, and substitute exercises that feel like skiing.

Instead of tennis and cycling, go to the mountains and hills, and take your Alpine ski poles. Speed-hike uphill, pumping your arms through a full range of motion like a cross-country track skier. To develop leg quickness, jog or run downhill. Slalom through the trees, planting your poles left and right as if you were actually skiing. Work on bounding as you come down the hill, low in a skier's crouch, weight going to the outside foot. For quadricep power, walk downhill slowly, carrying a weighted

Many fitness studios will tailor a training program specific to skiing. Clockwise from top left: Floor beam work for balance. Squats on toes for quadricep power. Yoga for flexibility. *(Bob Jonas photos)*

backpack. Hill work develops all three fitness components—endurance, strength and flexibility—and balancing skills, too.

In many parts of the country, fall weather turns nasty. When squalls and freezing rain force you indoors, you can use the Nordic Track machine to train for cross-country striding, and any number of home exercise devices to work up Alpine skiing muscles. The simplest of the Alpine exercisers is the Sport Cord rope, made of stretchy latex designed to

be inserted in a doorjamb and used with a waistbelt. A program of dips and steps simulates Alpine skiing. The Ski Legs exerciser is a platform for Alpine ski boots that provides resistance against which you can exercise the rotational muscles of the legs.

ALTITUDE SICKNESS

If you live at lower elevations, you may expect certain symptoms to turn up within the first twenty-four hours at a high-altitude resort: it's not uncommon to have insomnia, a general uneasiness, nausea, rapid heartbeat or tunnel vision (when peripheral vision darkens and all you can see is what's in the center of your field of vision). These are all the result of hypoxia—the brain simply isn't getting as much oxygen as it wants. The problem is that there's less oxygen in every breath you take, so less oxygen is getting into the bloodstream. The heart tries to compensate by pumping more quickly, to move more blood, but the fact remains that you can only get so much air into the lungs with each breath, and there isn't enough of it out there. If you fly from sea level to mile-high Denver, then hop in a smaller plane to go another mile higher to a Colorado ski resort the same day, you're asking for a smashing headache—in rare cases, even for life-threatening pulmonary or cerebral edema. But you may not be affected at all. Altitude sickness is one of those great medical enigmas. Exactly how the lack of oxygen affects the body to cause illness remains unknown. There are cases on record of hard-core mountaineers, accustomed to carrying heavy loads over 20,000 feet without distress, suddenly being struck with altitude sickness. And there are cases of unconditioned trekkers easing upward while Goliaths fall.

Acclimatization is the most important principle of going to high elevation. It's simple: go high slowly. When you get sick, there is one sure-fire cure: go to a lower elevation. If you're planning a ski vacation to the Rockies, you might consider first visiting a town built below 7,000 feet for a few days, and only later moving up to the major mountains with summits over 12,000 feet.

In addition to exercising before you go skiing, there are a number of things you can do to help you through the first three days of a high-altitude vacation with minimum discomfort.

First, lay off all alcoholic beverages during that time. If you aren't getting enough oxygen to keep the brain happy to begin with, you'll get befuddled on just one or two beers.

Second, drink plenty of nonalcoholic fluids. High, thin air is very dry, and when you're out in the sun and wind you'll dehydrate very quickly. Even a very small drop in the amount of fluid in the body dramatically lowers your ability to move oxygen through the lungs, into the blood and out to the muscles. Keep your fluid level up and it will help all the other systems to function. Get dehydrated and in the evening you'll feel hot and feverish—almost as if you have the flu. A corollary to this rule: Protect yourself from sunburn, which greatly exacerbates dehydration.

Third, eat a good breakfast, with lots of orange juice. Keep your blood sugar high. Eat plenty of green veggies to keep your iron intake healthful—your body responds to thin air by manufacturing more hemoglobin for the red corpuscles, which carry oxygen. The most important constituent of hemoglobin is iron. The faster you can take in iron, the sooner you'll adapt to the high altitude.

Fourth, don't overdo the physical exercise. Don't try to ski all day long the first day out, and don't try to dance the night away until several days after you *can* ski all day long. Instead, plan to linger over meals, enjoy the scenery, relax and exercise moderately. Enjoy. After all, it's a vacation.

Plunging downhill on Alpine skis. *(Sun Valley Co./Lindholm)*

6
Alpine Skiing

Skiing downhill commands attention because it is exhilarating. When we ski well, swooping in perfect linked carved turns, balancing sweetly against gravity and centrifugal force on a slender whip of a steel edge, then the whole body is engaged. In a turn, we can feel in the sole of the foot the set of the ski edges, the muscles of calf and thigh tense and release, the knee and ankle vibrate and dance. The back moves supply, relaxed yet strong, the shoulders roll into the momentum, the hands and arms sweep forward as if conducting a symphony for the skis. The sense of control with good downhill skis is so complete that this rush of speed feels safe and secure.

The sensations are intoxicating, addictive. John Kirschner of Sun Valley is a superb skier, who taught for nine years in the Vail ski school. Now, at forty-two, he's a happy, relaxed skier. "It's my favorite form of exercise," he says. John skis so efficiently that skiing is effortless. John loves the way skis glide under his feet. "I like gravity feed," he says. Gravity feed means John can slip off the lift and drop gracefully through the glades and bowls on Baldy. It's a sport of finesse, not power. John finesses life: as a hobby he builds fine wood furniture. He likes the way tools feel in wood just as he loves the way skis feel in snow.

When skiing with friends, John's concern for finesse surfaces. The ski instructor breaks out. "Let's work on your skiing a little," he suggests. Then he offers useful hints on using the terrain more efficiently. The pay-off is more speed, less work. A professional ski instructor helps students finesse the descent.

Market researchers say that almost fourteen million Americans say they are skiers. There probably are fourteen million people in the United States who have skied once or twice, but there are probably only about eight million people who ski regularly—say, ten days a year or more. Most of these eight million people who ski regularly at America's lift-served resorts learned to ski from a Professional Ski Instructor of America (PSIA), using the American Teaching Method. The ATM progression is a series of exercises and skills boiled down by the pros, after years of experience, into a versatile and efficient system. The goal is to help each student move easily and smoothly toward effortless, efficient skiing in all kinds of terrain. At different ski areas, individual instructors are free to adapt the ATM to suit local snow and terrain conditions, and—most important—to suit the temperament and talent of each student. It's a flexible system, but the basic elements are universal at American resorts: the new skier learns (in this order) to glide while controlling speed with a wedge, to turn with the wedge, to turn using a stem christie, a wide-track parallel turn, and a true parallel turn. From the stem-christie level on up, the instructor can take a student onto progressively steeper and more varied terrain.

The first-day lesson is called A Class, and the top students attend F Class. A student of normal athletic skills, in good physical shape, can expect to move from A to C level in three days of lessons. At that point he has acquired the skills to negotiate all of the easier terrain on the mountain, and can begin to consider himself an intermediate skier. In D class the skier acquires the foundation of the parallel turn; by the time he graduates to E class he can handle all the intermediate and advanced terrain on the mountain. In F class the student masters all terrain and all snow conditions. A good athlete can reach this level in sixty to ninety days on the snow—taking an occasional lesson, piling up practice miles in between. Learning goes faster if you can ski day after day, in solid week-long or two-week stints. New arrivals in ski towns often become expert-level skiers within a single season, skiing every day. But even if you ski only on weekends, you can improve significantly, and eventually reach the expert level, if you challenge yourself.

Let's follow a typical ski lesson. On the morning a skier shows up for the first A class, nervously carrying rented skis and shuffling along in awkward-feeling boots, a smiling ski instructor greets him and tries to pronounce his name correctly. The instructor also makes sure that each student is comfortably dressed and properly equipped—too often, be-

A professional ski instructor demonstrates before an Alpine ski class. *(Sun Valley Trekking/Brettnacher)*

ginners arrive with inappropriate boots and skis borrowed from friends. The class may have anywhere from three to ten students, but today we are four. "This morning," the instructor explains, "we will learn to glide, to stop and to turn. But first, we're going to get comfortable simply walking and sliding on our skis."

Our instructor today is Jacky—it's easy to remember because she wears a name-tag on her ski school uniform. In Jacky's beginner class this morning are Wilbur, a portly, sixty-seven-year-old man; his wife Irma, sixty-five; Benjy, a seventeen-year-old high school student; and Angela, twenty-three, who works for an advertising agency.

Jacky gets the group moving, moving, moving. She wants these neophytes to forget how awkward the stiff boots feel at first, and to become comfortable and well balanced. As she teaches, she constantly demonstrates, chides and jokes, keeping the atmosphere light and cheerful. Early in the day she learns about her students' athletic experience, their strength, conditioning and anxiety levels. Wilbur, recently retired, was a college football player back when football players wore leather helmets and no shoulder pads. Before that he played high school hockey. "I've always wanted to ski, and never had time to before," he says. He admits his knees might be a little weak from old injuries, but points out that "I still skate well." He grins like a kid on Christmas morning. Irma swims and plays a little tennis, but doesn't claim to be in good shape. "I'm just a good sport," she says. Benjy plays soccer on the varsity team. Angela likes aerobic dance, working out at least twice a week.

Jacky shows her students how to step into their ski bindings. They learn to glide comfortably on flat terrain as Jacky has them slip along, with and without poles, stepping in different directions and racing off to a target.

Wilbur seems a natural, but Irma is more tentative. Angela has trouble until Jacky gets her to stand tall, centered naturally over her skis and sliding fluently instead of hunkering and shuffling stiff-legged. Benjy is strong and manages to power out of his bindings a couple of times. He learns to be gentle, using very little upper body movement.

The Alpine skier's body is naturally centered and upright, with ankles and knees flexed forward.

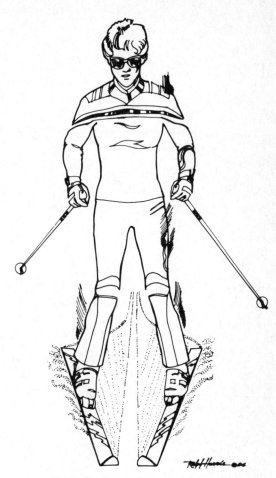

In the gliding wedge position, the skier places an equal amount of weight on each foot while brushing the tails of the skis out so that the skis form a wedge.

Next, Jacky shows her troupe how to climb on their skis and glide smoothly, in a straight line, down a gentle slope and across a flat area to a safe, easy stop. Skiers call the straight line down the slope—the line of gravity—the *fall line*. Jacky's students are now ready to learn how to slow down and stop during a fall line run by pushing the tails of the skis out so the skis form a *wedge*.

GLIDING WEDGE

• Find a gentle slope with a flat section at the bottom. Stand near the bottom of the slope. Use your poles to hold yourself in place and turn your ski tips downhill, so that the ski tips point down between your poles. Release the poles and glide, letting your skis slide to a gentle stop on the flat.

• Do this again. This time, as you glide, rock forward and back. Feel the pressure of your boot tongues against your shins, and of the boot back against your calves. Find a comfortable middle position, with the weight evenly distributed along the length of your foot. This is a balanced position.

• Try it again. This time shift your weight from foot to foot, and find a comfortable stance with the weight evenly divided between both feet.

• Move higher up the slope and keep your centered, balanced position as you glide faster.

• Now stand still, without gliding, on flat terrain. Push your skis out into a wedge, with the tips together and the tails apart. Feel how they rest on the snow. Notice how the edge angle changes as you go from a small wedge to a big wedge—the skis tip up more on edge as the wedge gets wider. The inside edge angle of the skis is the brake—more edge, more brake.

• Practice making big wedges and small wedges.

• Climb a gentle slope. Then, holding yourself in position with your poles, step the skis into a wedge pointing downhill. Release the poles and glide downhill in your wedge position.

• If the skis cross, push them apart with equal pressure or weight on both skis. The skis should be weighted equally and edged equally. You should be balanced.

• Try a smaller wedge and a bigger wedge. The smaller wedge glides faster, the bigger wedge slower. Find a wedge size that allows you to glide at a comfortable speed.

• Experiment some more. If you make the wedge big enough, it will slow you to a stop. Practice wedging to a stop while gliding straight ahead.

Irma has a little trouble here. She bends her right knee deeply, which puts her weight solidly on her right foot, so her wedge naturally produces a left turn. Jacky shows her how to stay centered, bending both knees simultaneously, equalizing the weight on both feet. "Now, you'll be able to wedge with both skis, evenly," Jacky says.

Within an hour, the group is able to control their speed easily going straight down a gentle slope. Now, they're ready to make their first turns so they can control their speed while descending from higher up the slope. In the wedge position, Jacky moves straight down the fall line, demonstrating how to weight the right ski to make a smooth *wedge turn* to the left.

WEDGE TURNS

• Find some flat terrain. Put on both skis and stand in the wedge position. Look at your skis. Notice that one ski points left and one points right—they seem to align with the direction you point your big toes.

• Still in the wedge position, put weight on the ball of your right foot by bending the right ankle and knee. Now

The skier demonstrates a wedge turn in this drawing. Starting from a natural upright position, the key to a successful wedge turn is to properly weight, then turn or "steer" the outside ski.

turn or steer your right foot toward the right big toe—the "inward" direction. The right ski swivels to the left. Do the same thing with your left foot, and you'll find the left ski goes to the right. This happens going down the mountain, too. Steer the right ski, you turn left. Steer the left ski, you go right.

● Put two ski poles upright at the bottom of the slope, about twenty feet apart. Climb up the slope and glide down the fall line between the poles in a gliding wedge. Turn the right ski slightly, straighten up, then turn the left ski slightly. Watch the poles, not the skis.

● Go back up the slope and make one big turn to the left, and keep turning left until your skis glide to a stop, pointing slightly uphill. Do it again, to the right. This complete turn is a more effective way to come to a stop than a "braking" wedge in the fall line. Notice that whenever you steer away from the fall line, your speed slows.

● Turn left, but don't stop. Instead, as your speed slows, straighten up and begin steering to the right. You are making *linked wedge turns*. If your skis look more parallel than wedged, that's fine too. You're ahead of the game. Remember to go back to a wider wedge if your speed feels too high.

● Go higher up the hill, and link more turns. As your speed increases, feel your weight fall naturally onto the turning ski. Turn or steer this weighted ski with ankle and knee flex. Think about steering or pivoting your foot, or about pointing your big toe in the direction you want to turn.

● Flatten the ski between turns by rising up gently into a tall, extended position. Rising tall takes the ski off its inside braking edge, allowing you to change direction and come down steering into a new turn with the opposite ski.

● Climb back up. This time keep the skis pointing across the hill, not down the slope. Push with your poles to start the skis gliding. Work your knees toward the slope—to the uphill side—to keep your ski edges in the snow. This keeps you from slipping down the hill. This glide across the hill is called a *traverse*.

Jacky asks Wilbur to try it. For Wilbur, today, everything is easy. He hasn't even fallen down yet. Irma makes the wedge turn to the left easily, too, just by going back to her right-foot mistake. Angela's first turn is sloppy but effective. Benjy overpowers his turn by leaning his body hard to the right, collapsing his right knee inward, and arrowing off downhill on the inside edge of the ski. He flops in the snow—it's the only way he can stop now—and asks, ruefully, "What did I do wrong?"

Jacky demonstrates again how properly to steer and weight the right ski. She tells Benjy to stay centered, bending his right ankle and knee gently while turning or steering his right foot. Now Benjy is able to turn smoothly.

After the class has made a couple of good turns to the right and a couple to the left, Jacky leads them to the bottom of the chairlift.

Riding the chairlift looks tricky, but the tough part is getting off at the top. Before loading, Jacky has her students watch experienced riders get aboard. Then she shows them how to slide into place, with skis pointing uphill, and how to wait with ski poles held in one hand, body half-turned away from your chair

partner so you can grab the chair with the free hand. She shows them how to sit down as the chair sweeps up from behind. Then she tells them what to do when they unload at the top. Now the class moves forward to the loading place, where a lift attendant helps each student load. Jacky goes first, riding with Irma, who is a bit timid. At the top, Jacky helps Irma ski off the lift, and then coaches the rest of the class as they unload.

Getting off the chair means simply standing up and pushing away, but it also means skiing down a ramp. It's no steeper than the beginner hill, but it's much narrower—there's no place to go but straight ahead, controlling speed with the wedge. But Jacky's class gets off with no trouble, and before lunch break she leads them down the hill three times, practicing turns and stops all the way.

After lunch the class gathers once again at the ski school sign. "This morning we learned two ways to slow down and stop, the braking wedge and the wedge turn," Jacky says. "This afternoon we're just going to ski for a couple of hours, practicing these wedge maneuvers, and we'll try to link our wedge turns together."

In two hours of riding lifts, it's possi-

A class in Alpine skiing. *(Gary Brettnacher)*

ble to ski several miles, even if you're a slow-skiing beginner. Jacky emphasizes speed control by changing the angle of the wedge: her skiers find they can slow down with a wider wedge, and speed up with a narrower wedge.

Comfortable with her students' control on the slope, Jacky begins to link wedge turns by emphasizing in her own movements the leg action of turning the skis. As she finishes a turn to the left she rises to a tall centered position and floats straight down the fall line, momentarily flattening her skis. Now she "steps" forward to the left ski, steering it to the right.

Without fanfare, Jacky continues to ski graphically in front of her class—step,

float, step, float. Her upper body is quiet, her hips centered, knees and ankles flexing as she steps. She makes short turns close to the fall line.

But Jacky is playful, too. She swings her arms through some turns, she "schusses" straight down the slope to a skidding "hockey" stop, she weaves up and down, she goes fast, then slow—all this on the beginner slope. Her students, watching and imitating this variety, quickly gain confidence in their ability to balance and turn on skis. While they may be steering with their upper bodies instead of using leg action in their turns, Jacky knows that as they go higher on the mountain—and faster—the rotating upper body will quiet down and leg action will become dominant. Right now, they're turning—and having fun.

By four o'clock, when the class breaks up, Angela and Benjy are bobbing happily around the hill, riding the gentle swells and ridges like gulls sitting on the waves. Wilbur is bubbling over, playing games—he has discovered, all by himself, that he can step from ski to ski, and with this technique has moved himself a day ahead in the learning progression. Irma is skiing smoothly and confidently, if more slowly than her classmates. "As long as I can keep Wilbur in sight I'm skiing fast enough," she tells Jacky. "Someone's got to look after that man."

At the end of the day, as the lifts are closing, Jacky tells her class that they're already B class students. "Wilbur," she says, "you could probably skip over to C, but that would mean leaving Irma behind. If you'd like, she can take a B class in the morning, then you can practice together in the afternoon and take a C class together the next day."

Early the next day, because the class is small and progressing rapidly, Jacky decides to teach a B class morning and a C class afternoon. In the morning she demonstrates and explains a "stepping into the turn" movement, followed by steering with the outside foot in the desired direction. She increases the speed, narrows the wedge and keeps her students close to the fall line while turning. This produces more and more wedge turns that skid at the end. Skidded turns are the next step in the progression.

In the afternoon Jacky takes her class to a slightly steeper pitch on the novice slope. From a standing position, she steps into her turn down the pitch, weighting and steering the outside ski with more intensity. This causes her skis to slide sideways, shortening the turn. This side-skid is called a *christie*. At the end of the turn her skis are parallel, rather than in a wedge position, and pointing slightly uphill. To feel their skis skid, Jacky asks her students to practice this *uphill christie*.

At first, Jacky starts her students at a low angle down the pitch. Then she has them start at progressively steeper angles, ending by skiing straight down the fall line before turning off into the christie. This progression is called a *fan* or *garland* exercise. It teaches students edge control, before and after skidding.

Jacky also helps them practice long turns and short ones, setting an easy obstacle course of traffic cones or ski poles. The class is growing in confidence. Jacky takes them to a longer lift, with slightly steeper terrain. Here the class works on varying the turns to match the angle of the hill: shorter, complete turns to control speed on steeper angles, longer, more gradual turns on gentler angles.

On the third day Jacky demonstrates the *stem christie*. She shows them how to slide just one ski into a wedge to start the turn. Moving just one ski-tail outward into a wedge, she says, is called a *stem*. After practicing the stem in a traverse, she leads them onto an intermediate slope for the first time.

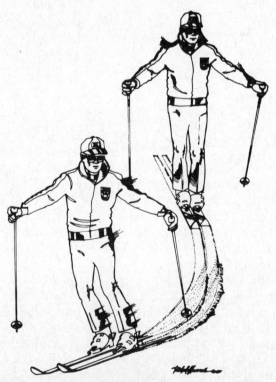

The "fan" or garland exercise, ending in a skidded turn (uphill christie), helps the student to learn edge control.

A stem christie turn begins with a stemmed uphill ski. The ski is weighted and steered as it swings to the outside of the turn. The knees and ankles are flexed deeply as the skidded skis are brought together.

STEM CHRISTIE

● Traverse across the hill but at a slight angle downslope. As you glide, push the tail of the uphill ski out into a stem, then bring it back parallel. Push it out, bring it back. On a broad slope, you should have room to do this several times.

● Try it again. This time, as you brush the tail of the ski uphill, rise up tall. As you bring the ski back into parallel position, sink lower by bending the ankles and knees. Repeat the exercise across the slope, then turn and try it in the other direction. Remember: Brush the *uphill* ski out into a stem.

● Try it again. This time, after you brush the tail of the ski out, stand on that ski and steer it into a turn. Turn to a stop with a smooth, controlled skid.

● Try the same turn in the other direction.

● Do it again. This time, think about bringing the skis back into parallel position as you enter the skidded part of the turn. Practice it in both directions, turning to a stop each time.

● This time, don't stop at the end of the turn. Instead, as you complete the turn, rise tall and stem the uphill ski to begin a new turn. Link these turns all the way down the hill.

For Jacky's students, the stem christie has evolved into a one-two-three exercise. One, stem the right ski. Two, step onto it, steering it to start a turn to the left. Three, "match" the skis—bring them back parallel. Then, do it over again on the left side: one, stem the left ski. Two, step on it to start a turn to the right. Three, match the skis. One, stem. Two, step. Three, match. One, two, three. One, two, three. "Oh, boy, we're cooking now!" yells Wilbur. On steeper terrain, the turn rounds out with a nice skid.

On the fourth day, all four students are assigned to a D class. Here Jackie adds to the stem christie the idea of *unweighting* to release the skis for a direction change. She demonstrates again how she rises up and "floats" between turns. She has the class rise tall to start the turn, then sink by bending the ankle and knee smoothly throughout the turn. Unweighting by rising up lightens the skis momentarily, helping to release the edges so the skis can be steered into a smooth skid. Keeping the knees bent allows her skiers to control their ski edges more accurately—either to continue skidding or to set the edge to prevent a skid.

At this point Jacky notes that Benjy is pushing on his pole for balance as he turns. So she introduces the pole plant as a timing device to begin the turn. "Plant the pole as you stem," she says. "Plant the left pole to start a left turn—think about turning around the pole." It takes a couple of runs before everyone has coordinated hands with feet, but now the stem christies really smooth out. "Notice where your weight is at the end of the turn," Jacky says.

"It's on the downhill ski," says Angela.

"It's on the outside ski," says Wilbur.

"They're both right," says Benjy.

"Correct," agrees Jacky.

"What do you mean by the outside ski?" Angela wants to know.

"It's similar to turning a sharp corner in your car," Wilbur says. "The weight goes on the outside wheels. Those are the tires that do the work. So, as you move through the arc of a turn, the weight goes outside because of centrifugal force."

"The outside ski that becomes the downhill ski is your controlling ski," Jacky says. "Vary the weight or pressure on that ski, you vary the edge. The more pressure or more edge, the more control."

With the idea of one-ski control, the students begin to step more aggressively into their turns. Stem-and-step christies become step christies. At this point the group begins to eliminate the last vestige of the wedge, beginning their turns with a parallel step. For stability and ease of movement, the parallel step is done with the skis in a *wide-track* position—separated instead of close together. Instead of counting "stem-step-match," the class is now using a two-count turn: "pole-step, pole-step," or "touch-turn, touch-turn."

That afternoon the group puts on some big miles on intermediate terrain. Jacky shows her skiers how to use gentle rolls and bumps in the snow to unweight the skis effortlessly. "The bumps are like the black keys on the piano," she tells them. "They look scary, but they tell you where you are and help you turn." As her students gain confidence, their skis are matching earlier and earlier. She encourages this. And they show increasing ability to vary the radius and speed of their turns. Most of the time, they are making *basic parallel turns*.

A basic parallel turn is a two-step motion: 1) rise up while stepping on your uphill ski; 2) sink down into the turn, firmly weighting the downhill ski.

BASIC PARALLEL TURN

● Begin by traversing across the hill. As you glide, step up onto the uphill ski, keeping it in the parallel position. Now, step back down onto the downhill ski, then up again. Repeat the exercise across the hill in both directions.

● Do it again. This time, as you traverse and step, face your chest downhill.

● Try it again, now gliding at an angle down the slope instead of traversing. This time, after you step onto the uphill ski, match your skis and steer both skis around into a turn. Finish the turn with a controlled skid to a stop, settling low by further bending the ankles and knees.

Try it in the other direction.

● As you complete the turn, remember to keep your chest facing downhill.

● Try it again. This time, step up onto the uphill ski, and simultaneously plant your downhill pole as you match and steer the skis into the turn. Skid to a stop with your chest facing downhill.

● Do it again. This time, instead of skidding to a stop, continue to glide, step onto the uphill ski and plant your downhill pole as you steer the skis into another turn in the opposite direction.

● Link these turns all the way down the hill.

Fifth day is E Class. "You're ready for the big words," Jacky tells the class. "How about *anticipation*? It's not so confusing as it sounds. It just means we get ready for the next turn by looking downhill to where we want to turn. When we're skiing downhill, the upper body faces downhill. That means we have to twist at the waist as the skis turn under us."

Jacky shows the class how positioning the upper body independently from what the legs are doing helps build an edging platform under the skis at the end of each turn, and helps the skis rebound off that platform, easily, into the next turn. By late morning Jacky is able to point out that Wilbur and Angela are no longer stemming; both are doing pretty fair *parallel* turns. She encourages them to skate from ski to ski to start their turns. "Skiers call it a *step turn*," she tells Wilbur. "You skate onto the uphill ski, then roll it over onto its inside edge to begin a new turn. You have to balance carefully against centrifugal force as the turn starts. It's tricky."

Not for an experienced skater. Wilbur tries it and instantly is turning twice as fast as the group. He stops to wait. "That's fantastic!" he says.

The step turn is an important advanced technique, but the exciting part of the lesson comes in the afternoon, when Jacky takes the group to try some powder.

"The key to being a versatile skier is to be able to ski on one ski at a time on hard snow, but shift instantly to skiing both skis together in soft snow," Jacky tells the class. "Think about skating on packed snow, and surfing in deep snow. In powder it helps to pretend your two skis are just one single platform, because if you try to stand on just one ski, it will

sink while the other unweighted ski rises, and you'll fall."

Jacky takes the group back to smooth intermediate terrain to practice skiing with the feet equally weighted. They stay very close to the fall line, where it's easy to weight both skis together. They unweight softly from turn to turn. "Pump the knees together!" Jacky says. "Stay centered and flow from turn to turn."

The next step takes the class into the six-inch depth of powder on the edge of a run, where they can try a couple of turns and sweep back onto the smooth groomed trail to regain their balance. After one tumble, Jacky cautions Angela: "Don't try to muscle those turns. Turn the skis together. Let the skis complete the turn by themselves."

In deep snow, the students soon find that speed is a problem—the skis won't slide forward on gentle terrain. To get up enough speed to make turns, the slope has to be fairly steep, and you have to make fairly short turns, straight down the fall line. The skis sink out of sight deep in the turn, and bob to the surface between turns, when you're light.

"It's like flying!" Angela says. "It's like being a porpoise, bouncing up out of the snow after every turn!"

After several weeks of practice, Wilbur, Irma, Angela and Benjy are ready for F Class, the top of the ATM progression. In F Class, skiers work on mastering very difficult terrain, or on racing technique. These are all advanced techniques, the basis for expert-level skiing. Jacky takes the class to some real expert terrain—short and smooth and wide, but very steep. "The trick here is to reach way downhill to plant your pole," she advises. "That's real anticipation. You put your upper body down the hill—and that takes the weight off your skis so they can follow along, into another turn." There are a couple of ski-tangling tumbles, but the skiers are excited, especially Benjy.

At the F level, the group splits up. Wilbur and Irma choose to join a racing class, where they can compete against people their own age (Wilbur is confident he can whip 'em all). Angela wants to spend more time skiing in deep powder, and Benjy wants all the steep, bumpy terrain he can find. Jacky finds Benjy a class to join, and gives Angela a private lesson in the fresh snow.

The class has discovered the weight-less exhilaration of Alpine skiing—to them skiing has become a kind of dance. Every skier gets hooked on the sensations of skiing, but each skier may be addicted to a different feeling—the trembling of the skis on the snow, or the rush of wind in the face, or the giddy semi-controlled fall of steeps. Jacky's students, like many other skiers, have found delight in the rhythms of Alpine skiing, the alternating left-right-right-left-left-right compressions and rebounds. It's the sort of movement you can sing to, and it's an oft-overlooked element of ski technique. Get the rhythm and you too will be a graceful skier.

Professional ski instructor Mark Pearson critiques two students at a destination ski resort. *(Sun Valley Trekking/Brettnacher)*

7
Cross-Country Skiing

Unlike the Alpine skier, who skis mostly lift-served slopes, the cross-country skier is free to roam about all of the white world of winter.

The cross-country skier may move swiftly over machine-groomed trails set on level fields and rolling hills. This is *track* skiing. At other times he may ski off the track, through the unbroken snow of meadows and woods. This is *ski touring*. Or he may set out to find hillsides and try *cross-country downhill*.

TRACK SKIING

Most new cross-country skiers start out by taking lessons on the track. The track is a wide, groomed trail made by a snow-cat or snowmobile towing a heavy sled. The sled, equipped with one to four pairs of iron skis, cuts precise grooves in the smooth, firm snow surface. Each groove is just slightly wider than a ski, and your skis follow the grooves easily, like wheels on railroad tracks. The tracks are used for *diagonal stride* skiing.

Skate skiers use their skis just the way ice skaters or roller skaters would, pushing the feet outward in a widening V pattern to accelerate forward. Because the skis point outward in the V, they don't follow a groove in the track, so the left side of the groomed trail is left smooth and firm. Both the strider and the skater concentrate on keeping up a smooth rhythm, letting the groomed trail do most of the steering.

You'll find groomed cross-country track courses at special cross-country ski resorts and at many lift-served ski resorts. The special cross-country areas usually offer much more tracked terrain. For example, California's Royal Gorge cross-country resort grooms 225 kilometers over 62 trails. You can ski from lodge to lodge, sampling 500 kilometers of trails in northeast Minnesota's lake country. Major Alpine resorts like Aspen, Colorado and Sun Valley, Idaho, offer extensive mileage, too. Seven different touring operations groom over 140 kilometers of trails at Sun Valley. At these places a skier can spend a week on groomed trails alone.

The track skier uses the lightest kind of skis and boots—the skis are far slimmer than Alpine skis, and the boots look almost like featherweight running shoes. The heel is free to rise off the ski as the foot articulates up and forward off the ball of the foot. The toe of the shoe is attached to the ski by a lightweight clip of steel, aluminum and plastic. A single ski, with its binding, may weigh less than a pound, a single boot under 12 ounces.

The reason for the light weight is that on each stride the skier lifts a foot into the air behind him—less weight means less work.

Fast track skiing is a lot of work—it's like running, without the jarring impact on each step. Track skiers often wear a thin, skintight racing suit because they burn enough energy to keep themselves warm without thick insulating garments. The track skier stretches out in a graceful, rhythmic kick, release and glide on each powerful stride. Done properly, it's a wonderfully smooth motion, so smooth that chronic injury in track skiing is very rare. There is no runner's knee, tennis elbow or bowler's wrist to contend with.

Most exercise authorities name track skiing as the best conditioner for cardiovascular strength and general muscle tone. It's a fast, exhilarating sport, too. A strong track skier can glide around a firm course at 15 mph—much faster than a distance runner can move. And all of this action occurs on a balance beam: the typical track ski is just two inches wide.

Let's look at how a strong track skier may adapt his technique to suit the terrain. We'll start by watching the diagonal stride. In most still photographs, you'll see the skier balanced on a single ski, the body and one arm reaching forward, the other arm and one leg stretched behind. The position looks like a dancer's arabesque. Shift from a still shot to a moving film and watch the legs scissor quickly to create a powerful downward pushoff or kick from the ski, and the skier floats into a long glide on the opposite ski. The action is called a diagonal stride because the left leg moves forward with the right arm, the right leg forward with the left arm—literally, diagonal corners of the body work together. Meanwhile the skis flash forward and back,

The diagonal stride. *(John Plummer)*

alternately, following the grooves in the track.

As you watch, you may see the skier shift gears, from diagonal stride to double poling. Now most of the forward power comes from the arms instead of the legs. The body moves up and down like a piston; the skier is erect as he reaches far forward to plant his poles.

With a bend coming up on the trail, a fast skier will shift to another technique. One ski flashes out of the track groove onto the skating lane, and the skier skates off this ski with a muscular sideways thrust, accelerating around the curve. One ski remains in the groove—the skier is skating on one side only.

Watch the skier step out of the grooves entirely, skating with both legs onto that smooth skating lane. The V-skate, using the most powerful muscles of the arms and legs, lets the skier move faster than he was able to in the track grooves. The skating steps are long and smooth—until the skier starts climbing a hill. As the hill grows steeper, the skating steps grow shorter and choppier until the skier is jogging, skis angled off in a wide V or herringbone to prevent backsliding.

At the crest of the hill the skier skates a few steps to regain speed, and as the trail drops into a long downhill glide the skier settles his skis back into the track grooves. To minimize wind resistance in the glide, the skier crouches into an aerodynamic tuck, torso resting on the tops of the thighs, elbows held in front of the knees. Toward the bottom of the hill, now moving fast enough to make his eyes water, the skier rises and moves one ski out of the groove again, checking his speed with a braking wedge. Going around the corner at the foot of the hill,

A cross-country track skier charges up a hill. *(John Plummer)*

that wedge becomes a wedge christie and then the skier is skating again, maintaining momentum onto a long flat section.

SKI TOURING

When you leave the track, adventuring across natural snow, you are truly skiing cross-country, as did the farmers and villagers who used their skis for daily transportation in Scandinavia and the upper Midwest for generations. Today, this more basic form of the sport, on ungroomed snow, is usually called ski touring (or tour skiing—take your pick). While track skiing is a sensational workout, ski touring is a quieter, less intense, more contemplative sport. The tour skier stops often to rest and to appreciate the fragile beauty of the winter landscape— lovely hoar frost and mysterious animal tracks in the snow surface, ice crystals dancing in the sunlit air, the gracefully snow-draped trees.

Those old-time skiers set out on the snow simply to get from farm to farm or town to town, and today touring may

In the marathon skate, one leg remains in the track, the other skates to the side. *(John Plummer)*

simply be a means to get from one place to another. You can tour from inn to inn between Vermont hamlets, or follow a hut-to-hut route in Norway's midnight sun country.

But tour skiers don't have to go into deep snow. If you'd prefer not to break trail, you can choose to stay on the groomed track. Tour skis will work on the track, and until very recently most new touring skiers learned the sport on set tracks. Touring skis are slightly wider and heavier than track skis, making them easier to balance on, but they do fit into track grooves easily. Because of the extra width, which keeps a tour ski from sinking like the Titanic in deep snow, you can always leave the track for the woods and fields.

To control this slightly wider and heavier ski, especially where the snow is deep and soft, tour skiers use a supportive lightweight boot with a laterally rigid sole. The boot often comes over the ankle, both to offer more support and to help seal out snow (use nylon gaiters whenever the snow threatens to come over the boot-tops).

Because the equipment is easy to use and because you can go almost anywhere on easy terrain, ski touring is for the whole family. Mom, Dad, the kids, Gram and Gramps can participate. The family retriever or spaniel will want to follow along, too. You don't have to wait for the lifts to open or travel to a groomed trail. Ski in the backyard, in the city park, on a golf course or in the woods and fields near home. Skiing can be as easy as slipping out the back door.

Mrs. Jonas, sixty-seven, does just that. Each winter she sets her own track, alongside a lane between houses, through a cross-buck pole fence and into a stand of big, horny-barked cottonwood

trees to the frozen banks of the Wood River. There's always something new to be seen along the river. One very cold morning the ice fog from the river wound into the cottonwoods, and the squawking ducks on the ice couldn't see her approach.

"The slough was completely frozen over, and the ducks were waddling around on the ice, slipping like buffoons," she recalls. "Then out of the mist, wings spread wide and feet outstretched for landing, another flight of ducks came skimming toward the flock. As they touched down on the slick surface, a few of the newcomers managed to stay upright, webbed feet scrabbling, wings flapping. Most of them just flopped over, skidding along on one folded-up wing, quacking in surprise until they hit the snowbank. A few tumbled, rolling like feathered bowling balls into the group waiting on the ice, scattering them like— well, like duck-pins. The squawking! The snow and feathers flying! Not one duck was hurt, but I nearly died laughing!"

CROSS-COUNTRY DOWNHILL

As recently as 1982, Alpine skiers viewed the telemark turn as an exotic spectacle. Today it's common to see telemarkers arcing gracefully down lift-served Alpine runs, and thousands of dedicated Alpine skiers have adopted downhill cross-country skis and the telemark turn into their repertoires.

Ken, 29, an ex-surfer, is typical of the skiers who found the telemark captivating. "I love Alpine skiing," he says. "I want to get my downhill runs in every day. But I needed something new. I tried monoskiing and found it limiting. Then one day I saw this guy doing a crazy turn, and I chased him down. It was a telemark. I've been free-heeling ever since. I learned to free-heel parallel quickly because it's a lot like parallel skiing with Alpine gear, but telemarking was different. I had to start all over, as a beginner."

The rebirth of the telemark turn is one of the most interesting chapters in modern skiing (see Chapter 8 for a more complete discussion of telemarking technique). Born in an era when there were no lifts or grooming of any kind, the telemark turn has provided a way for modern skiers to move easily through the backcountry.

Sondre Norheim and his friends in the Telemark region of Norway needed a way to descend steep untracked slopes on their heavy, highly cambered, edgeless wooden skis. They had only floppy workboots and leather bindings. The combination was hardly the right one to transmit leg action into the powerful edging forces necessary for downhill skiing control. But Norheim found that two unstable skis could be scissored into one long arc, giving the skier a powerful rudder to steer the skis through a graceful turn.

He did this by thrusting one ski forward and one back, genuflecting on the rear ski and stretching the arms out sideways for balance. The forward ski could now be steered in the direction he wanted to turn, and the rear ski followed like the back wheel of a bicycle. It was a graceful, stable turn, especially effective in difficult deep snow which otherwise resisted steering movements.

When American skiers first tried riding ski lifts with fiberglass cross-country skis—in the mid-1970s—they discovered how frustrating it could be to control a steep descent on light free-heel equipment. On a slick, packed slope, the problem was even worse. Today the cross-country downhill ski is built as a lighter, narrower Alpine ski, with the same kind of sidecut and steel edges for good turning control. The telemark boot, like Alpine boots of earlier years, is a stiff leather shoe that comes over the ankle. Racers even use rigid plastic cuffs. The big difference between the telemark ski and the Alpine ski today is in the binding—the telemark skis with the heel free to lift.

That free heel gives the cross-country downhiller the option to ski parallel or telemark, as snow conditions and terrain dictate.

TRADITIONAL CROSS-COUNTRY TECHNIQUE

When you first take up cross-country skiing, you'll learn the traditional kick-and-glide diagonal stride. Diagonal stride has always been the core technique of cross-country skiing—you'll use it on the track, while ski touring, and in the backcountry to move on the flat and uphill on telemark skis. It's easiest to learn on a groomed track, with the help of a competent instructor using the American Teaching Method (ATM). Ski schools and instructors belonging to Professional Ski Instructors of America (PSIA) use this system.

You'll start on a section of flat, groomed terrain, set with track grooves. Your instructor will first lead you through a series of warm-up stretches, and tell you something about your equipment and how to use it. You'll probably start off on a wider light touring ski, which is easier to balance on and pro-

The "wagon wheel" exercise helps the beginner develop a sense of balance on cross-country track skis.

vides a good grip when pushing off your back foot into the diagonal stride. The first day starts with getting a feel for balancing on the skis. Start by doing this simple exercise:

• Face the "hub," marked by a hole poked in the snow, with your ski tips touching the hub. Now step the tails of your skis around in a complete circle to make a wheel around the hub (the marks your skis make in the snow are the spokes). Try it in both directions, clockwise and counterclockwise. When it feels comfortable, try it again with your ski-tails fixed at the hub and stepping the tips around. Should you fall, use your poles, crossed on the snow, to provide support while you get back up (see photo).

When you're sliding around comfortably on your skis, you're ready to step into the groomed track where your instructor introduces the *diagonal stride*. The diagonal stride is a natural stride. Its name is taken from the fact that the arms and legs move in opposition to each other—just like normal walking. The object of a good diagonal stride on skis is to achieve glide.

• First, try to diagonal stride in the track without using your poles. Make your movements soft. Push off the left foot and stride forward onto the right ski. Balance all your weight on the right ski and glide momentarily. Now push off this ski and stride forward onto your left ski. Hold the glide for a moment, then repeat; and again. Push off, stride, glide.

• To lengthen your glide, increase the vigor of your movements. Think of your arms and legs as widely swinging pendulums. Really flatten the ski from which you push. Push down and kick away as if you were accelerating a scooter. When you're striding forward, imagine yourself kicking a big beach ball down the track with the lead foot. At the same time stretch your torso forward as if leaning into a stiff wind. This enhances the forward extension necessary when

To get back up from a fall, bend forward to your knees and use crossed poles to help support you as you rise. *(Wood River Journal)*

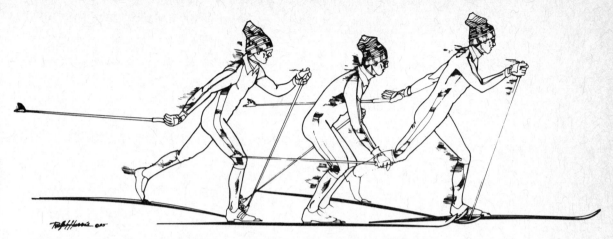

The classic diagonal stride technique is used both for the groomed track and on firm snow surfaces off-track. An exaggerated forward stride follows a strong push-off or "kick" from the opposite foot.

shifting weight from ski to ski in order to achieve glide.

When you feel balanced and are comfortable without poles, begin to work with pole technique. Correct use of the poles will lengthen your glide because you can now add arm power to leg power.

● For a correct pole plant while striding, let the pole drop and lightly seat its tip in the snow forward of your opposite foot (right pole tip drops ahead of the left foot). Your hand should extend well forward of the pole tip, so that the force can be applied immediately to the pole for forward momentum.

Now, pull down on the strap and as you slide even with your hand, push the pole backward, with a complete followthrough. Your opposite arm should now be swinging forward to plant its pole on the other side.

Stride briskly, but don't stab at the snow—seat the pole firmly but smoothly. The forward-arm swing makes an arc parallel to the ski track, not hooking across the chest.

● Now coordinate the pole action with your push-off from the ski. As your timing and balance improve, your kick will become more powerful and your glide longer. If your arms and legs move together, robotlike, a quick jog down the track reestablishes your natural rhythm.

Leaning too far forward into that wind will result in a slower recovery from ski to ski, as does excessive arm swing.

A correct pole plant helps power the diagonal stride in cross-country track skiing. After making an angled pole plant, pull down on the strap, then release it as you pass the pole.

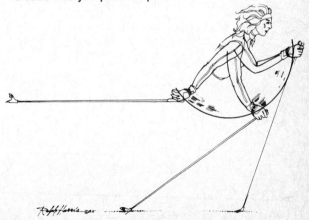

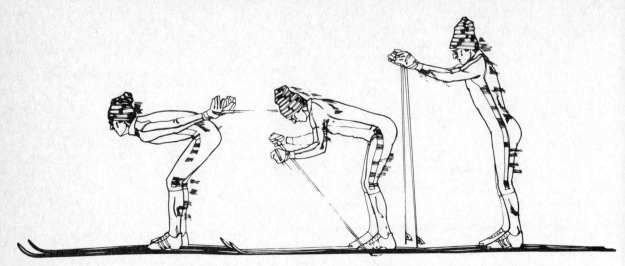

Double pole technique propels the cross-country track skier along sections of the track too fast for diagonal striding.

Make sure your weight transfer to the gliding ski is complete. A centered position and smooth movements will help you develop better timing and balance, and you'll be able to recover more quickly from small mistakes.

Mark Pearson, a member of the elite cross-country demonstration team of the PSIA, offers this advice on learning the diagonal stride: "The average skier with no previous skills or conditioning will achieve a glide satisfactory for a lifetime of track skiing in a week of practice and lessons."

When the skier is moving too fast to effectively diagonal stride on fast snow or sloping track, he or she uses *double pole* technique. The double pole motion duplicates that of the two gandy dancers pumping the hand car down the railroad tracks, except the down motion of the arms in track skiing continues all the way through and behind the body. Because the feet remain stationary, the technique requires a lot of arm and upper body strength. However, once momentum has been attained, it is easy to maintain that momentum. It's easy to learn the double pole, too.

● Standing stationary in the track, feet parallel, reach forward with both arms projecting your torso forward at the same time. Now plant your poles simultaneously near your ski tips. They should be upright rather than angled. Pull down on the straps, pulling yourself forward with your arms and shoulders through the planted poles without moving your feet. As you pass the poles, push them away to the rear, arms swinging freely. Let your upper torso compress until you are horizontal to the ground from the waist up, then raise up, and extend your arms forward to repeat the cycle.

The two most common errors in double-poling are to overextend the arms and to compress too far at the waist. A good tempo will help establish the correct reach; keeping your eyes down the track will prevent you from compressing your upper torso past the horizontal.

The double pole can be combined

with a kick. Instead of keeping your legs still when you reach forward with both arms, try pushing off with one leg, then with the other. Then try kicking with the same leg each time, or double-pole several times between kicks. This kick-and-double-pole sequence is a good technique for sections of the course too slow for double-poling alone, and can function as a restful intermediate technique between the stride and the double pole. Watch an experienced track skier or racer come off a gentle downhill glide and begin striding off across a long flat section. He'll probably mix the double pole up with some kicks, until his speed drops to where the diagonal stride becomes the most efficient technique again.

To ski uphill requires still another technique. If the hill is not too steep, and

The double pole combined with a kick. *(John Plummer)*

The herringbone technique enables a cross-country track skier to ascend steep hills. *(Wood River Journal)*

if you've used the right wax, often you can just blast up the hill using your diagonal stride. If you slip a little, quick jogging steps will get you over the top. But if the hill is steep, your kick or jogging won't be effective. You'll have to use the *herringbone*.

● Separate your ski tips so that your skis form a wide V, and walk or jog up the slope on the inside edges of the skis. The steeper the slope, the wider the angle of the V must be, and the harder your arms and legs will have to work. Where the slope is very steep (in touring, for instance), you may have to resort to *side-stepping* up the slope. It's like walking up a staircase sideways, with the uphill edge of each ski set deeply in the snow so you don't slip downhill.

Going downhill in tracks, to increase your speed, lower your body into an aerodynamic *tuck*. In this position, the hips are lowered almost into a full squat while the upper body folds forward from the waist over the thighs.

The step turn is a classic technique to negotiate corners on a track trail. It is also useful for low-speed turning off-track. In left photo the skier comes into the turn on one ski, his body low; he then makes a short step to the outside ski (middle) and steps back again to the inside ski (right), alternating the steps until rounding the turn. *(John Plummer)*

Maybe you don't want to go faster. To slow down, brush the tails of your skis outward, putting them in a V or *wedge* position (See illustration page 65). This, as in Alpine skiing, puts the skis on edge—the wider the wedge, the more edge is applied and the slower you'll go. Obviously, the wedge position requires you to step your skis out of the track.

Turns at the bottom of a descent may be accomplished several ways: at lower speeds, try a step turn or wedge turn. At higher speeds, use a parallel or telemark turn.

A *step turn* is a "soft skate" motion without much edge applied. You can practice it on the flat. As you push off the outside ski, pick up the inside ski and point it in the new direction of travel. As you step down on the inside ski, pick up the outside ski. The steps are continuous from ski to ski until the new direction is reached. Keep your hands held low, and transfer the body weight to the stepped ski slowly and smoothly.

Wedge and *parallel turns* are executed just as they are on Alpine skis (see Chapter 6). The outside steered ski is weighted and edged according to the braking control needed.

SKATING TECHNIQUE

Track skiing's new movement, the skate, exploded onto the recreational cross-country track scene in 1986. First developed by world class cross-country racers in the early years of this decade, skating has been in the wind for some years. The first racer to use the technique extensively was the American Bill Koch, who won the cross-country World Cup championship in 1982 by skating past his diagonally striding competition.

Skating is undeniably the fastest way to get around a groomed track. In the diagonal stride the ski stops at the end of every glide and is momentarily kicked back. By contrast, a skated ski moves forward continuously, the "kick" coming off the inside edge of the ski.

There are two skating movements: *V-skating*, in which you skate with both legs, and *marathon skating* (see lower left photo, page 79), in which one ski stays in the track while the skated ski, out of the track, is used as the pusher. A marathoner may skate to just one side at a time, but will change sides from time to time, if only to rest the power leg.

The V-skate is classified in two ways, according to the timing of the pole plant. In the *V-1 skate*, double poling occurs every other skate; with the *V-2 skate*, double poling occurs with every skate or step-down of the ski.

Skating requires more upper body strength and better overall balance than traditional striding. "Skating is sweat, a racing technique," says Bill Koch. "It's not necessarily for everyone."

The first time you try skating, you may find it exhausting. But Mark Pearson encourages new skaters to persevere. "When I first began to experiment with skating, I believed the energy demand was too great for it to be an effective technique," he says. "Now, after skating entire fifty-kilometer race courses, I think skating is actually easier on me. I don't feel as spent, even after short races. It's a question of building up the support muscles as you learn the technique."

Look at the sequence photos on pages 88–89 of Bill Koch V-skating. Four things stand out about this powerful technique: 1) the complete forward extension of the torso in making the pole plant; 2) the complete weight transfer from ski to ski; 3) the leg thrust off an edged rather than flat ski; and 4) the complete compression of the torso after the pole plant.

In order to give his students the feel of the lateral movement of skating, Pearson has them start skating by just traveling with the skis in a V position on the smooth lane next to the track. Weight transfer is almost automatic as the skis travel laterally. Balance over the skating ski comes more automatically too (because of these natural tendencies, skating is often used as a weight transfer exercise for diagonal stride students).

Skating equipment is very important. Too often skiers try to learn skating armed with 75 mm boots and wide wax-less tour skis to help with balance. "Heavy equipment makes skating nearly impossible," Pearson says. "Given the physical demands, a light waxable ski that is stable for the skier and light shoes are essential."

The tourer or in-track skier who has chosen a light waxless ski mated with a shoe/binding system (other than the 75 mm norm) does not have to buy new equipment to learn skating. If you like to alternately tour and "jog,"—and are not interested in sheer speed—the equipment you already have should be satisfactory for all track techniques, including skating.

If you do purchase skate skis you will discover that they are waxable. That does not mean that you have to learn waxing because skating, as we have described, does not require a grip wax for the kick; the kick comes from pushing off on the edge of the ski. You can ignore waxing and still achieve glide. However, waxing maximizes the glide, making skat-

ing more *fun*—you're able to slide along with less effort. Please refer to Chapter 9 for a complete discussion of waxing.

The important rule to remember when beginning to skate is not to hurry your movements from side to side. Give the skated ski time to glide, being sure that it is flat and not on edge. After gliding, roll the ski over onto its inside edge to create a platform from which to skate (thrust) to the opposite side.

Edging skills for the skating "kick" can be practiced easily with one ski in the track, the other ski out of the track in the marathon skate position. Get the feel of rolling your skate ski ankle to the inside and placing the ski on its edge. As the ski comes onto the edge, push off with a double pole movement. Now switch to the other ski.

To develop timing, balance and good edging, Pearson stresses basic step turns, and skate turns practiced in the track.

The basis of the step turn, as we have previously described, is to pick up the inside ski tip and step in a new direc-

tion. Stepping is continuous from ski to ski until the new direction is achieved. The skate turn is executed on the same basis, except the tip of the inside ski is picked up while pushing off an edged outside ski in the skate position.

By not using your poles during early skating maneuvers, you will focus your initial efforts more fully on your leg movements. However, your arms should

To get the feel of the lateral movement of skating, start by simply traveling in the skate lane with your skis in the V position. *(Wood River Journal)*

In this photo sequence, 1982 Nordic World Cup Champion Bill Koch demonstrates the V-1 skate. *(Gary Brettnacher)*

swing naturally during the push-off in the skate. If balancing is a problem, use your poles for added support. In the beginning, the marathon skate may be easier for you to work with than the V skate.

A good double pole technique is important to skating. In fact, some noted trackmen see skating as an extension of double pole technique.

The way the double pole plant is executed in skating is significantly different from the diagonal stride technique. Because skating splays the skis to the side, the poles cannot be planted opposite each other at the ski tips. Instead, the pole plant is staggered to prevent entanglement with the skis. A staggered pole plant means that one hand is planted higher than the other and in the direction of the gliding ski (See Koch sequence above). Because the skater shifts most of his weight to the high pole he works longer off that pole.

Since most skaters are V-1 skaters, the staggered pole plant results in the development of a power side. It is impor-

tant, however, to pole off *both* sides to develop strength and versatility, whether V-skating or marathon skating. Another possibility is to become a V-2 skater, planting the poles on every skate.

While double-poling is relatively easy in the marathon skate, you may find it awkward in the sideways motion of V-skating. This is why the V-1 skate or pole plant every other step—as demonstrated by Koch above—has evolved. The rapid fire poling of V-2 skating requires real timing finesse.

Timing is very important in skating. Inexperienced V skaters often roll the ski over onto its edge and start the leg push too early. As Koch demonstrates in the photo sequence, the double pole should be complete, or nearly so, before the push off begins. Good skaters, during the change over from one ski to the other, time the pole plant to coincide with the touchdown of the skating ski to maximize glide resulting from poling.

One major problem for new skaters attempting the V-skate is taking short steps, and not completely transferring body weight from ski to ski. As a result, they ski down the lane ducklike, feet apart, achieving very little glide. "The tendency to skate wide [stepping the un-weighted ski down too far away from the gliding ski] is a result of poor balance," says Pearson. "The well-balanced skater is able to swing his unweighted ski in close to his gliding ski as he moves it forward to step down."

One painful result of skating too wide can be landing face first between your skis in a split. If you're having problems with the splits in V-skating, return to the marathon skate. Concentrate on swinging your skate leg close to your track foot as Pearson demonstrates in the photo at the right. Now go back to the smooth lane with a slower pace, swinging your free ski within a foot of your weighted skate ski as you prepare to step down into the glide.

The long length of skating poles is striking. Use poles 10 cm longer than the poles you use for traditional striding in the track. The extra length allows a superior forward extension of your body and a longer pull-push with the pole. The net result is greater propulsion and more speed.

If the extra length of skate poles is too much for you at first, you may have to work gradually to a longer length. Also, double check that you are standing erect during the transition from one ski to the other, and that you are extending yourself far enough forward during the pole plant.

Despite the physical demand of skating and the awkward feeling early on, Pearson believes skating is easier to learn than diagonal stride technique. He cites how close the finish times of citizen racers are today using skate techniques. When diagonal stride was the primary racing

To help avoid a forward fall while skating, swing your unweighted ski close to the weighted ski before gliding on it, as Mark Pearson does here demonstrating the marathon skate. *(Wood River Journal)*

technique, times were spread more. "A lot of striders were not really proficient at the technique," he says. "Waxing played a role too. With skating, waxing is much less a science."

You can negotiate sharp turns on flat sections of the track course with the marathon skate; longer turns can be strided around in-track on the gliding ski while holding the kick ski back.

On the hills, skating is superior to striding. A skater often can continue right over low hills without losing glide (see photo on facing page). On steep hills, the skater will have to change over to the herringbone just like the strider to finish a climb. But again, the skate technique may get you farther up the hill. The skater uses the same descent techniques as the strider.

What is the future of the skate technique? Skating is termed by some a revolution in cross-country skiing, surpassing the introduction of fiberglass skis. It is perhaps the most important change in the history of cross-country skiing. Race politics are in turmoil because traditional diagonal striders control the race world's governing body. "Freestyle" races have been instituted to accommodate skaters; "classic" races favor striders.

Equipment manufacturers are quickly developing skating skis. One example is the Rossignol Nordic Concept ski. The RNC is the first ski with an integral boot/binding. The ski has a top ridge down the ski's midsection with a built-in binding fixed at midridge. The grooved track shoe fits over the ridge. The system accommodates the lateral stresses of skating better, giving the skier more stability, better balance and a stronger ski.

Cross-country skiers using skate technique can easily glide up gentle slopes. *(John Plummer)*

Pearson and the rest of the National Demonstration Team are working on an ATM manual incorporating skating. Interestingly, Alpine teaching axioms—pressure (weighting), edging and turning—will be stressed more than ever in cross-country techniques. Skating is helping to close the gap between the Alpine and track ski worlds.

Skating will surely change. Koch, for example, sees the marathon skate as a transitional technique that will disappear. Pearson believes the pole plant every other step (V-1 skate) that Koch demonstrates so graphically in the photo sequence on pages 88–89 will disappear. He thinks a double pole every step (V-2 skate) will become the norm. He also predicts that ski skating will come closer to ice skating speed technique, the body more compact and low to the ground. One thing is certain. The cross-country world will adjust to the skating revolution because skating is a new, faster way to have fun on skis.

CROSS-COUNTRY DOWNHILL TECHNIQUE

The learning sequence for free-heel parallel is exactly the same as the Alpine parallel progression (see Chapter 6). However, remember that your heel is free and that you do not have the stability that Alpine equipment provides. You must stand softly on your entire foot. Movements must be liquid and precise. Because of these balance prerequisites, free-heel parallel turns are excellent exercise for Alpine skiers as well.

If you are an Alpine skier attempting free-heel downhill for the first time, you will need to practice the feeling of the wedge turn on cross-country skis before proceeding. Then practice the stem christie and the parallel turn. All of these turns are easy to master on a beginner or intermediate packed slope in good snow condition, once you are able to relax on the less stable cross-country equipment.

Telemarking packed slopes requires more strength than free-heel parallel, and certainly more strength than skiing downhill with conventional Alpine gear. The telemark position itself and the lack of ankle support in cross-country downhill equipment requires significantly more leg strength to hold the edge.

A lift-served skier can ski comfortably all day in Alpine gear, but will rest frequently while telemarking in cross-country downhill equipment. Only on soft snow and in powder will the telemark turn be as easy as Alpine skiing. For this reason many cross-country downhill skiers take to the backcountry where cross-country skiing—indeed, all skiing—had its origin. It is in the backcountry chapter that we examine the telemark technique in detail.

Cross-country, skiing's oldest incarnation, is changing dramatically. Developments in cross-country have injected new blood into the sport, bringing more people to skiing than ever before.

8
Backcountry Skiing

From the top of the lift, look around at the neighboring peaks. Marching to the horizon, the mountains are huge and snowy, with no lifts and no skiers. Why not ski where the snow is untracked and the slopes uncrowded? Why not leave the groomed tracks and trails for untouched wilderness? Why, in a vast white land, should you be limited to a crowded, postage-stamp piece of winter?

You shouldn't. Thousands of skiers use the backcountry safely and comfortably each winter. You enter the backcountry the moment you strike off from the plowed road, headed for an alpine meadow on your cross-country skis. You ski backcountry each time you check out with the ski patrol for permission to make a last run down the backside of your favorite mountain.

Skiing this near backcountry is essentially road skiing. The cross-country tour skier loops out from the road or returns on the same route to his starting point. Skiing from a summit pass down into the valley is the most popular kind of backcountry downhill skiing. Skiers leave a car on the valley road, drive to the top of the pass and ski back down.

The backcountry skier can usually be on the way to some private summit while lift-bound skiers are still waiting for a parking spot. At the top of the pass,

backcountry skiers emerge from their cars, zip up their gaiters and put climbing skins on their skis. Lunch packs are shouldered, bindings clipped shut. Soon

Porpoising in and out of powder snow while telemark skiing in the far backcountry. *(Sun Valley Trekking/Brettnacher)*

a friendly line of skiers moves up the shoulder of the mountain. They snake along the ridge, taking turns breaking trail through the new powder snow.

A run down through seamless powder snow is an exquisite pleasure, well worth the climb. Powder caresses, embraces. The skier sinks into the first turn, enveloped by the white ocean, then rises like a dolphin, powder pluming, to tip gently into a new turn, again plunging into the powder sea.

The trip back to the summit goes faster the second time, as the skiers no longer have to break trail—they simply follow their own upward track. Backcountry skiers move at a more relaxed pace than do lift skiers—they ski slowly, relishing each turn in the powder, instead of blasting feverishly through mogul fields. They stop often to admire the view, instead of standing in lift lines.

While the pace may be slower, backcountry skiing is a more intense experience. It's not that the powder is better than you'll find on the lift-served mountain. It's the wildness! Slopes are not groomed or carefully cleared of hazards. The skier can sneak through a crook of trees, pop out into a clearing for a few turns in the fall line before dropping into a deep ravine or launching off a rock outcrop. The line of descent follows the natural terrain. Skiers duck under huge fir limbs, slalom through aspens, and roller coaster over downed snow-covered tree trunks. Telemarking through this stuff is wild fun.

The telemark turn is to the backcountry skier what parallel is to the Alpine skier. Often, the telemark is more stable in mixed snow conditions and while skiing with a pack than parallel technique. It is wonderful in powder.

The first element of the movement is to genuflect deeply on the uphill ski, as the downhill ski moves ahead, so that together the skis are one long bow. In genuflecting, the telemark skier is bent low in the very quick of the powder, surfing on his long bow. Then, the feet move; the skier rises, the other foot shoots forward and a new turn begins.

There are several ways to gain access to the backcountry without touring to the area you want to ski. Snowmobiles and snowcats are used as transportation in the backcountry, but the most popular and successful mechanized way to reach the virgin powder of the backcountry is to fly. Helicopter skiing takes one to the high peaks to ski untouched snow fields, without the work and time of climbing into the backcountry.

Helicopter skiing was first introduced in the mid-sixties in the deep powder country of the spectacular mountain ranges of western Canada. A gritty Austrian mountain guide, Hans Gmoser, built a mountain lodge as a helibase in the remote Bugaboo range. He banked on a growing pool of skilled skiers seeking the powder experience, ever in short supply on lift-served mountains.

Gmoser's advertisements showed his helicopters setting down atop vast powder fields backdropped by soaring peaks, with skiers threading endless figure eights down the white sea below. For a guaranteed number of vertical feet of skiing per day and a week's lodging, his charge was a hefty sum. He waited. Such is the siren call of powder snow that skiers soon came from around the world and continue to this day.

Now, most of the major western U.S. ski resorts have heliski operations that can put you in backcountry powder in minutes. And the snow is every bit as good as one finds in the legendary Canadian mountain ranges.

A big lift-served mountain like Sun Valley's Mt. Baldy offers 3,000 vertical feet of skiing from summit to valley. In a helicopter, you and a group of friends can bag 30,000 vertical feet, or the equivalent of ten big mountains, in a single day. And, by using the helicopter at the resorts, you always have the option of lift-served skiing if the powder changes to windpack overnight or if the risk of avalanche is too great on a given day.

SKIING CONDITIONS IN THE BACKCOUNTRY

Wind, sun, temperature and time quickly go to work on new fallen powder (see Chapter 2). Wind can pack new powder into a leg-catching slab that rafts on top of the snowpack. Temperature rising above freezing during the day and the beat of the sun on south and west slopes will produce a melt/freeze suncrust on the surface.

But even if fresh powder snow is not available in the backcountry, touring is always possible. East and north slopes often harbor pockets of great powder long after snow on southern and western slopes has metamorphosed into a rigid hide.

As the skiing season progresses, and the sun appears higher in the sky each day, a new phenomenon occurs in the mountain snowpack: corn. Suddenly, the entire backcountry is transformed into a magic carpet upon which to stride, skate and ski downhill with boundless energy.

Touring on corn is child's play, simply delightful. At no time of the year will you find the backcountry so accessible. Snow is no longer a barrier; it is a paved highway. This is the time of super glide

in the backcountry. On corn, you sail across the surface of the snowpack. All the brush, holes, rocks, trip and stumble of the summer months are sealed beneath, the way smooth.

Backcountry skiers who tour corn snow leave town before first light. They want to ski while the corn is gleaming and firm, before the sun softens and melts it. It is best to tour up a gently rising valley. On the downhill, you'll find yourself zipping along. An occasional double pole or skate maintains the momentum. It's a dizzying experience to plunge into a thicket of pine, to slalom your way through while maintaining your glide.

Downhill skiing on spring corn snow in the backcountry. *(Bob Jonas)*

SKIING CORN: A BACKCOUNTRY EXPERIENCE

Early on a balmy mid-April morning a group of backcountry skiers at a western resort drive off to the nearby mountains for a morning of exhilarating skiing on pristine slopes. At the site, they strip to shorts and T-shirts, apply sun tan lotion liberally and attach climbing skins to their cross-country downhill skis. Despite the early hour, the air is warming fast. The skiers want to be on top while the corn snow—arguably the fastest and smoothest of all snow conditions to ski on—is in peak condition. Later in the morning the corn will turn to slush under the warming rays of the sun.

After an hour of climbing the skiers reach the summit. It is a picture perfect day with an azure sky and not a trace of wind. To the south, foothills trail off into a low plain. To the north is a rim of white peaks. The light would be blinding if the skiers were to take off their sunglasses. The skiers stand on top of a large open bowl with a perfect fall line below them. As they peel off their ski skins water bottles are passed. They cannot linger, as already the corn is beginning to soften.

Down the steep upper section of the slope the skiers make parallel turns. As the slope becomes less steep, they switch to the telemark, genuflecting gracefully on bent knees.

Two and a half hours after leaving town they are back, the morning's run a cherished memory to carry them through the day.

Skipping across snow bridges and following the twists and turns of a creek is more fun yet. And on even a slight downhill you can coast for a long way.

You can also ski corn at night after the freeze tightens up the melted snow. A moonlit tour on corn is a magical experience.

THE FAR BACKCOUNTRY

Beyond the near backcountry is the unknown adventure of the far backcountry. Far backcountry skiing is wilderness skiing. There are two ways to get into the far backcountry—trekking in on skis or flying in.

A bush plane fitted with skis, or a helicopter, can drop a group of skiers off at a remote hut. From here they can explore further or ski back out.

Hut skiing is the easy way to know the far backcountry in winter. A hut, a day's tour away, may be linked with other huts strung along the wilderness frontier. Skiers use the huts as overnight bases to penetrate the designated wilderness, which by law contains no permanent structures.

Hut skiing is a European tradition, and was brought to a few places in this country by European ski instructors at American ski resorts during the thirties

Backcountry skiers before a temporary backcountry hut, a Mongolian yurt. *(Bob Jonas)*

On the Sawtooth Haute Route, Idaho. *(Bob Jonas)*

and forties. It died out in the fifties with the boom in lift-served skiing, but today a few entrepreneurs are bringing hut skiing back.

Huts can be either temporary cozy wilderness shelters like those in the Sun Valley backcountry, or permanent cabins, such as those found along the Tenth Mountain Trail and Hut System between Vail and Aspen in Colorado. In either case, the huts are an island in a white world providing spartan but comfortable facilities.

Backcountry hut skiing is an opportunity for all ages to experience a special winter adventure. Hut skiers love to get away from it all. Sharing the close quarters of a snow-bound hut with old friends

or new ones is part of the appeal.

The most exciting backcountry ski experience—and a crowning skiing achievement—is to ski a wilderness haute route (high route) in one of the great western ranges.

A high route ski trek along the spine of an Alpine range is a skiing spectacle. On a wilderness haute route the skier combines cross-country and downhill skills continuously. Skis, as in the beginning of skiing's history, are used to gain access to the Alpine terrain. Today's new, sophisticated equipment allows you to ski downhill in virgin snow on a peak never before skied. By day you travel through or over a variety of snow conditions; at night you sleep in the snow. On your first haute route trip you'll learn more about mountains and snow than you could discover in a lifetime on groomed trails.

In America, we call such routes *wilderness* haute routes because the much better known *European* haute routes, like the classic route between Zermatt in Switzerland and Chamonix in France, are dotted with large stocked huts. A few can be reached by ski lift. In a wilderness haute route, you are entirely self-supported. There is no easy access or egress (air drops in legislated wilderness are illegal except in Alaska). Your shelter is a snow cave or light backpack tent. The preparation involved and the skills necessary are more exacting. Most likely you'll encounter no other party—the experience is qualitatively different!

The Sawtooth Haute Route in Idaho is an example of the kind of high routes now being established in the mountain ranges of the American West. It begins in the little hamlet of Stanley, seventy miles north of Sun Valley. In late April, Stanley is a sorry mess of mud-paved streets. But way up beyond the town the white peaks of the Sawtooth soar into the clear blue sky. There, spring is still at least two months away.

The first day on the Sawtooth is the toughest, a long ascent to get out of the low country. The skier must climb approximately 3,500 feet over nine miles. Men and women alike carry pack loads of fifty to sixty pounds containing food and fuel. Over the next nine days, six more major ascents are made as the route zigzags along the spine of the range. The placement—pretour—of a food cache is necessary to complete the seventy-mile wilderness route.

Jagged peaks capped with cornices frame the skier's route. The passes are slots pinched between rocky towers, the canyons deep and narrow, the Alpine lakes hemmed by steep mountain walls.

The Sawtooth Haute Route requires eight separate snow camps. Two nights are spent in a camp near midrange; a single night is spent in each of the remaining camps. Generally, skiers tour cross-country for four or five hours a day. The remaining time is devoted to downhill pleasure skiing and making camp. Making camp means digging snow caves or tent platforms, and, if the group is large, even a snow kitchen for the entire group.

Early in the skiing season the route is too dangerous to ski because it crosses or follows the edge of several major avalanche tracks. While springtime does not assure safety, the snowpack has consolidated to the point where it is generally safe.

A spring haute route carries the skier through every kind of snow imaginable. A north slope may be all powder, while from the same crest to the south may be a marvelous corn. You'll find everything else in between, as well—wind crust, slab, suncrust, ice, slush and avalanche deposition. A foot of new snow at night means midseason powder next morning. But by noon the new snow may have turned to the consistency of thick soup, getting progressively wetter as the sun rises higher. Wet snow avalanche "music" is as integral to the haute route skier's experience as the coming ashore of waves is to any beach visitor. Snow slides down narrow chutes and off steep slopes, the thunder of avalanches filling the mountains.

Wind on the crests may whip new falling snow with such intensity that the skier will have to shield his face, while 2,000 feet lower in the sheltered valley it floats down, as airy as dandelion seed parachutes. Temperatures gyrate. One moment the skier may be skiing bare-chested, sweltering in the sun; half an hour later he may have to bundle up against a full-scale blizzard. This is winter wilderness. A haute route is as different from a day on the lift-served mountain or the track as the December Pacific surf pounding the beach at Mauna Kea is from Walden Pond.

Some ascents are rhythmical, the skis sliding easily, the pack well balanced. Others, in deep powder, are laborious and exhausting. Ascents on steep hard corn may keep you on the very edge of your skis. A kick-turn here is a delicate maneuver—if you fall, you'll rocket back down the switchback trail to the bottom.

The climbing is tough, but the reward is fabulous skiing in spectacular, silent wilderness.

BACKCOUNTRY SKIING TECHNIQUE

You'll find that much of your movement while touring in the backcountry is a sliding walk. You're intent upon making progress on the trail, rather than making speed. Touring is in many ways similar to a summer hike—you're looking at the country, moving at an enjoyable pace. When breaking trail in deep snow in the backcountry, the skier uses a high forward kick; when the snow is less deep, a sliding walk is more practical. If a trail is broken and the way clear, or you are skiing corn snow, you can utilize a diagonal stride or skate technique.

You may decide you want to be a "ski hiker" only, that you are not interested in learning downhill technique when you tour the backcountry. If so, sliding along with an occasional vigorous diagonal stride may be the only technique you will need. But if you hike up a slope or hill,

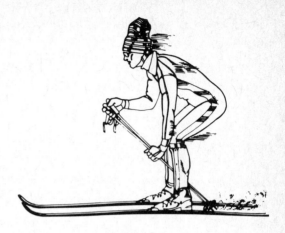

you will have to come back down. Coming down, you have three options—and in deep snow, taking off your skis and walking is not one of them.

1) You may control your speed as you descend back down the trail by putting your climbing skins on your skis. They act as brakes in dry snow. However, on hard snow they may glide too fast.
2) You may use your poles together between your legs as a brake lever. Pull up on the handles, push down midshaft as you force the tips and baskets into the snow behind you (see above). If the pole brake does not slow you sufficiently, then combine it with a wedge position and/or your skins.
3) Your third option is to traverse back and forth down the slope.

When snow conditions are poor, accomplished downhill skiers use all these techniques for downhill control. If they want to stay on a trail, the pole brake may be the only practical option, because backcountry trails are often too narrow for turning.

The downhill skier in the backcountry, whether a cross-country or Alpine skier, looks for two snow conditions—powder and corn. And he'll want to learn

The telemark position. To control your speed while initiating a telemark turn, step your outside ski into a half wedge, then stride forward onto that ski into the telemark position.

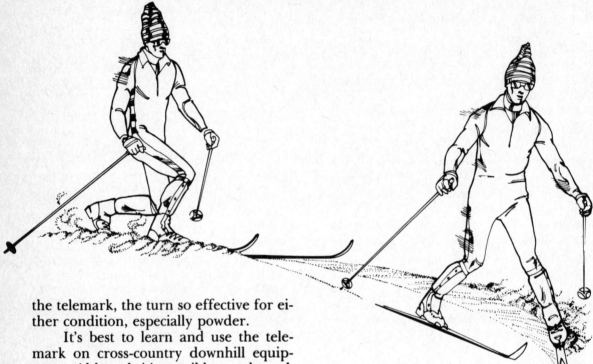

the telemark, the turn so effective for either condition, especially powder.

It's best to learn and use the telemark on cross-country downhill equipment. Although it's possible to telemark on an Alpine touring system, the turn is neither so effective nor so enjoyable as its execution on cross-country skis.

TELEMARK TECHNIQUE

"Coming down in the telemark position, kneeling; one leg forward and bent, the other trailing; his sticks [ski poles] hanging like some insect's thin legs, kicking puffs of snow as they touched the surface and finally the whole kneeling, trailing figure coming around in a beautiful right curve, crouching, the legs shot forward and back, the sticks accenting the curve like points of light, all in a wild cloud of snow." (From "Cross Country Snow" by Ernest Hemingway)

The telemark is easier to learn on a groomed slope. Start at the cross-country touring center. All centers have a beginner slope on which they teach telemark technique. Many have access to lifts so that you can get practice in before going into the backcountry.

On the flat, practice the telemark position. Advance the left foot, bending the knee and ankle, and dip the right knee, nearly touching the snow. Now switch legs, sliding your right foot forward. Your front foot should be flat, while the back foot rests on the ball of the foot. Your upper body should be quiet, hands low (see illustration above left).

The telemark is a physically demanding position. It takes strength; you can feel the strain in your legs. A shallow telemark position is easier on the legs. Move to a groomed track with a slight downhill and begin striding. On the forward gliding ski, come down into the telemark position. Hold until the glide ceases, then switch to the other ski. Keep alternating, trying the high, intermediate and low telemark positions.

Now go to the beginner slope and ski directly down the fall line, keeping your skis parallel. Near the flat, come down to your telemark position just as you did while striding on the track. As you move across the flat, switch to the other leg. Keep doing this until you feel comfortable, each time getting into your telemark position earlier and more often. Be sure that your body position before executing the telemark is neutral and upright—you should momentarily be coasting. Don't switch from leg to leg too rapidly; you will lose your balance.

Now you are ready to try the telemark turn. On the beginner slope, as you reach the flat, with your right foot advanced in the telemark position, steer gently by pointing the right foot and knee to the left. As the skis turn to the left, keep your upper body quiet and facing straight ahead, as if you were still headed directly into the fall line.

Try it again from an *intermediate* telemark position, right foot forward and pivoted to the left, left foot straight ahead or pivoted only slightly. You will find yourself turning to the left. Now check your position and refer to the illustrations on the preceding page:

1) Your feet should be relatively close together, approximately one foot separating the back of your front heel from the toe of your back foot.
2) A portion of your weight should be on the ball of the back foot; do not place all your weight on the forward foot (but do remember that weight commitment to the forward ski is important). Experiment with balancing your weight between both feet until you find a comfortable position.
3) Your forward ankle should be flexed, not locked and rigid. If your ankle is locked, it means your weight is too far back, and you haven't committed yourself properly to the forward ski.
4) Your upper body should be facing straight ahead. Do not rotate your hips to follow the skis as you turn. Your upper body should remain motionless.
5) You should feel your outside or right foot (in a left turn) steering (guiding) the turn. The right foot and knee should point strongly to the left.
6) Your hands should be down and forward, not way out to the side. Use your arms to make slight balance adjustments. But always keep them forward.
7) Your eyes should look downhill, rather than following the direction of the turn. Remember, you're skiing a mountain, not a turn. You will be aware of the direction of your turn with your peripheral vision at the same time you are searching down the mountain for your next turn location. Don't acquire turn-to-turn tunnel vision; you will only bump into other skiers.

On the slope, continue practicing single telemark turns in each direction.

Now you're ready to link turns. At this point we defer to your PSIA (Professional Ski Instructor of America) instructor. You will need a teacher's watchful eye and instruction to attain fluency in linking telemark turns. The instructor will be able to smooth out sequential positions, introduce the pole plant for timing and help you make the mental and physical adjustments necessary. Here, however, are some notes regarding telemark turns:

Alpine and telemark skiing require the same basic technique: centered body, pole plant inside the turn and weight transfer to the outside, controlling ski.

While skiing deep powder snow, stay close to the fall line, weighting and pivoting both feet as one.

1) Always maintain control while turning. Initiate your telemark by stepping your outside ski into a half wedge to control the speed, then stride ahead on that ski. The wedge position not only helps your control but sets up the outside ski, on edge, to come across the inside ski (see sequence illustration). If you find you are still accelerating, begin the telemark from a full wedge.

2) Finish a turn in complete control. Rise to an intermediate, neutral position, then in slow motion stride your opposite foot forward into the next turn and once again sink into the telemark position. Pivot your outside foot and knee in the direction of the turn.

3) Practice striding from outside ski to outside ski with greater authority and confidence.

4) Set up two bamboo poles in order to turn around, one downslope from the other, near the fall line. That will help you look ahead instead of down at your skis and enhance proper timing of your movements. After successfully turning around two poles, try four. Then try the open slope.

It's going to take longer to learn the telemark than parallel turns. How long will vary widely among individuals. Balance and timing are more critical than for parallel skiing. You must remain centered over both feet even though they are separated on a long axis. Your stride forward, weight commitment and steering to turn must be accomplished simultaneously. If you are tentative when striding into the telemark, and your weight is back, you in effect have no turning power or edge control. If you commit all your weight to the lead ski you lose the stability of the "long bow"—the two skis turning together as one long ski. Worse, your back leg and ski, unweighted, may flop around and even cross over your lead ski *behind* your foot, causing a spill.

Alpine downhill experience is not necessarily an advantage in learning the telemark. Many Alpine downhill skiers have difficulty breaking out of parallel technique and into the telemark position, while skiers who have only cross-country track experience slide comfortably into the telemark.

For Alpine skiers who want to incorporate the telemark turn in their downhill skiing repertory, the basic technique is the same. The body is centered over the feet, weight transfer is forward to the outside, controlling ski, and the pole is planted to the inside of the turn.

With practice you will adapt to the special balancing requirements of telemark skiing. Done well, it is the most sensuous of downhill maneuvers—it remains popular because it feels so good.

SKIING POWDER

Powder ski techniques are the same for parallel and telemark at basic levels. Two important premises apply to skiing powder: first, you do not need to control your speed the way you do on packed snow. You're skiing *through* snow, not over the snow surface. The snow depth itself will slow you down. Second, weight your skis equally rather than putting more weight on the outside (downhill) ski.

In deep powder you will not need to use your ski edges. Instead, you will be looking for the steepest slopes just to enable you to attain sufficient speed to make turning possible. On gentler slopes, you may find yourself schussing straight down the fall line just to get through

deep powder without stopping. If, however, only a few inches of light dry powder rest on a base of firm packed snow, you will need to apply edges in your turns as in packed slope skiing. Most powder conditions fall between the extremes.

In deep snow, hug the fall line and stay equally weighted on your skis as if they were a single surfboard. The ability to weight equally is enhanced when your feet are closer together. In deep powder, if you weight the downhill ski the way one does in packed skiing, the ski will sink deep into the snow, while the unweighted ski will rise to the top. At that point you may feel as though you're riding a wild bronco, legs flying. Inevitably, you will end up face down in the snow.

It's important where you stand on the skis, in relation to the kind of snow you are skiing. On packed snow you should be forward on the balls of your feet, driving your weight toward the tip of the skis as they lie on their sidecut and carve a turn on the edge. In powder you're on the entire foot. You do not need an edged turn; you want to keep the tips floating and the skis surfing. However, don't stay on your heels in powder—your quads will begin to tire from the effort, and your ability to stay equally balanced on the skis will suffer. If you're having difficulty floating, try to pick up more speed by keeping your turns right in the fall line and very shallow as opposed to wide and swinging. The type of skis you use will make a big difference too. A "soft" or uniformly flexible ski is best for powder, as opposed to a stiffer ski. And a wider ski floats better than a narrow one.

Powder skiing, like racing and bump skiing, takes practice. Find a slope where you can ski close to the fall line and yet be in complete control. The powder should be deep enough to hold your descent to a comfortable speed. Here are some tips:

1) While skiing the fall line keep your upper body quiet, weight evenly distributed on both feet, feet together. Now rock gently on your feet backward and forward. Feel what your skis are doing when you make these motions. Find a comfortable position for the powder condition you're skiing while standing evenly weighted on both feet. The tips of the skis should be floating on top of the snow as you move downslope.
2) After making your pole plant, *pivot both feet together* while turning. Settle your hips downward at the same time.
3) Don't move too far out of the fall line. Rise up and float back into the fall line.

Here are two things to keep in mind: if the powder is deep, stay in the fall line and surf with both feet. If it's shallow, edge softly in the fall line, weighting first one foot then the other.

Why does the telemark turn work so well in powder even though the feet are not together? Primarily because the freedom of the heels allows you to glide one ski past the other to create a long narrow bow. At the same time you're able to get low on the bow over both feet. The long bow has unusual fore-and-aft stability in the deep snow, far more than the parallel ski position. The free heel also allows the back foot to come up on its ball and rudder the bow. The front foot is flat, steering the bow. You're centered between them.

The balancing act in telemark is delicate. What you gain in fore-and-aft stability, you lose laterally. The feet apart position does not provide as solid a base as having your feet together. Many skiers compensate for the lack of lateral stability

Sometimes the only way down a backcountry slope is to kick steps down and/or be belayed on a rope. *(Bob Jonas)*

while telemarking by spreading their arms wide. Most experienced skiers try to keep their hands down and forward—this will make you a more balanced skier. Still, telemarkers are an independent lot, and more than one experienced skier spreads his arms out.

After mastering the telemark and powder snow techniques, you're ready to ski downhill in the backcountry.

Remember that in the backcountry you'll be climbing and skiing steep hard slopes and learning to ski with a heavy pack. Skiing with a heavy pack is like ice skating with a child on your shoulders—except you're going downhill and have to react quickly. Unless snow on the descent is good powder or corn, ski down slowly. Traversing and kick-turning are often the best way to descend. If you do turn, the telemark is excellent for skiing with a heavy pack.

It is not unusual for backcountry skiers to find themselves upended ingloriously while skiing with a pack. Pack skiing is like walking a tightrope—you must be balanced and precise. Use only a frameless pack with a snug fit.

A hazard exacerbated by pack skiing is hitting hidden rocks and wood with your back knee while telemark skiing in powder. It's a good way to hurt a knee. Many telemarkers use knee pads because of this. Always survey the slope for submerged obstacles below the surface. They often advertise themselves as bumps in the snow. Try to avoid them as you head down the slope.

If you find yourself on a steep backcountry slope with a hard snow surface, it's best to take off your skis and continue down using kick steps with your boots.

Plunge the skis into the snow, tail first, to use as handles ascending or descending. A fall on hard snow on a steep slope can be dangerous if there are rocks and trees along the way. And falling on corn crystals is like being rubbed with no. 36 grit sandpaper.

If you know that your route will pass over and down steep slopes or cornices, bring along a 9 mm climbing rope. On a cornice descent, the skier who skis out on the edge to check cornice stability should be belayed with a rope.

You should rope up, as well, whenever you ski a glacier, in case one of your party falls into a hidden crevasse. Practice this technique on a glacier in an instructional situation before backcountry skiing on a glacier field.

The backcountry skier regards cornices with extreme caution. *(Bob Jonas)*

FOOD, SHELTER AND NAVIGATION IN THE BACKCOUNTRY

Food planning and packing is an enormous job on a long haute route. One ten-day Sawtooth route required sixty-two pounds of freeze-dried food for fifteen people. That doesn't seem like much until you realize that each freeze-dried package averaged four ounces. And there were more dried and whole footstuffs plus volumes of tea, coffee and chocolate drinks.

In addition to a higher carbohydrate intake, you'll need more fat than normal on a haute route. Because fat is utilized more slowly by the body, it will keep you warm at night and energized on the trail. Plenty of snacks and drinks along the trail help too—hydration is very important. There is a tendency in the cold snow environment to drink less, especially when you have to melt snow for water.

Don't carry any extraneous cooking equipment. Food and equipment should be organized for groups no larger than four. On a long haute route you'll probably have to cache some food and fuels along the route before the tour begins unless air drops are possible. The cache site must be carefully selected, marked and buried *deep* to protect it against wild animals.

Camp near lakes when possible. Overflow water, seeping up through lake ice cracks or from inlet streams, pools on the ice below the snow cover. It saves time and fuel that would be spent in melting snow for water.

Shelter usually consists of a light backpack tent or snowcave. There are three types of snow shelters: above surface shelters, such as an igloo; recesses, such as a trench or a slope chamber that has one side open; and closed caves. The

A slope snow chamber, with a sleeping platform and cooking bench. *(Bob Jonas)*

last begins as a trench, with a tunnel cut into the trench wall. The tunnel leads back to an elevated chamber dug within the snow on a slope.

The cave is time consuming and wet to construct. An igloo takes even more time to build unless you have the benefit of hard slab snow which can be cut easily into blocks. Trenches and chambers are quick, easy to fashion and less messy to construct. Ultimately, the type of shelter you decide to make will depend on the weather, how tired you are when you begin to dig, the parameters of the site and how long you intend to stay at the site.

Alpine haute routes have enough visual horizons that by and large you should be able to get by with a U.S. Geological Survey seven-and-one-half-minute quadrangle topographic map. But if you are touring a dense forest, in open country or an area plagued by day-long storms, you should carry and be able to use a compass as well. While many American ski-adventurers have never used one, European guides consider a pocket altimeter indispensable for accurate navigation in poor visibility.

It is best to go in groups of four people into the far backcountry. That makes

A major avalanche. The avalanche wiped out a band of aspen trees and swept across the road. *(Reid Dowdle)*

trail breaking comfortable when the snow is deep, and provides enough people to help in an emergency. In the case of an accident, one person can remain with the injured skier while the other two make the fast trip out for help. More than four to six people increases the probability of an emergency and alters the wilderness experience.

You should respect your fellow skiers with whom you share the trail. Under winter conditions, this is especially critical for a long trek of ten days or more. It is best to choose a group with skills and equal physical strength. Often, physical endurance turns out to be more important than skiing finesse. Attitude is even more important. Agree on pace, skiing objectives, side trails and the quantity and quality of food before you leave.

Skiing the far backcountry is an extraordinary experience, but requires far more knowledge and skills than a day spent on the tracks or lifts. It is best to ease into backcountry skiing gradually. Track skiing or lift-served mountain skiing is vastly different from a wilderness haute route. Make your first trips with an experienced group or a skilled guide.

BACKCOUNTRY SKIING SAFETY

Once you're beyond the umbrella of safety provided by the ski patrol on the lift-served mountain or at the tour center, you risk two very real hazards in the backcountry: snow avalanche and cold exposure. The first is a killer not even the most expert skier can predict with absolute assurance. The second is insidious: hypothermia disorients you so that you don't perceive the danger. Frostbite is another cold exposure danger.

Most near backcountry ski tours are brief trips of a half day or less. They are undertaken in favorable conditions and terrain. Because of this 95 percent of the time one is able to tour along without being aware of the hazards and safety precautions necessary in backcountry skiing. But skiing the winter backcountry without being prepared is like Russian roulette; what you don't know can kill you.

The possibility of avalanche can be just as serious at the edge of the road as in the far backcountry; and an accident victim may suffer cold injury before he can be evacuated. *Do not ski the backcountry unless you are prepared for the hazard of avalanche and cold exposure.*

Always avoid the backcountry during a big storm and the day after a heavy snowfall. Before departing on a trip, check with the local Forest Service office or responsible land management agency for the backcountry avalanche forecast. Don't ski alone, and always let someone know your itinerary and planned time of return. Downhill skiers are more at risk than the tourer because they ski steeper terrain and thus are more apt to release avalanches.

The day of the tour check your avalanche transceiver batteries. An avalanche transceiver is an instrument not much bigger than a cigarette pack. It emits a distinct high frequency beep on transmit. The beeper allows rescuers to locate a victim buried in an avalanche.

Even if you are only going out for the day, always carry a day pack that contains drink, snacks and extra clothing, as well as a few tools and replacement parts

to repair a broken binding. You should also include a first aid kit and a pad plus tarp and sleeping bag to protect an injured victim from hypothermia while waiting for evacuation. Carry a lightweight shovel with which to dig out a buried skier and use ski poles that can be made into an avalanche probe to help locate the skier.

You should be aware of existing snow conditions. Always be alert for tension in the snowpack while skiing, especially that telltale "whumping" sound. The "whump" is the settling of the snow pack. Fissures may rip across the snow surface. The sound alerts you that there

Backcountry skiers dig a pit on a slope, checking for instability in the snowpack before skiing the slope. *(Bob Jonas)*

has been a mini-snowquake; it is the grumbling of the pack adjusting to stress upon it and it is a sure sign of instability. Steer clear of those places.

At the slope down which you decide to downhill ski, dig a deep pit and look at the snowpack in profile. Probe the line between layers to look for poor bonding: smooth suncrusts, ball-bearing-like pellets (graupel) or snow that is sugary, without moisture and texture (depth hoar). Take temperatures at each layer, to look for a "TG" (a temperature gradient) snowpack (see also Chapter 3, "The White World"), especially sharp from bottom to top, which indicates instability. An equitemperature snowpack (EG) reflects stable bonding between layers. Learn to do a shear test: cut a column of snow free on the sides at the face of the pit wall. Gently ease a shovel down behind the column. If suddenly an entire layer shears easily from the column, it is another sign of instability. Get a copy of *Snow Sense,* a booklet on avalanches published by the Alaska Department of Natural Resources. It's available in most mountaineering equipment shops. It's small enough to carry with you into the mountains. But the classic and comprehensive treatise is *The Avalanche Handbook* by Ronald Perla and M. Martinelli, Jr. (U.S. Dept. of Agriculture Handbook 489, U.S. Government Printing Office).

Last, listen to your inner voice, the instinct that senses danger. If you feel uneasy, take heed.

Skiing among the trees as opposed to skiing on an open slope is not necessarily a guarantee of safety from avalanche. Safety during tree skiing depends upon the shape of the terrain above the woods—an avalanche starting higher up can easily run down through the forest—

as well as on snow conditions. Always ski down one at a time the first time a slope is skied. Even after a dozen runs, remain alert. An avalanche may release on a slope even after the slope has been skied several times.

Consider your backcountry route, whether touring or downhill skiing, carefully. Stay away from gullies and obvious avalanche tracks. Stay on ridges (but off cornices) both on the ascent and along the crest. When a ridge route is not possible, stay close to dense stands of trees. Cornices should be given a respectable berth. Corniced slopes, especially north and east exposures, should be given extra attention before crossing. They may be loaded guns.

When wind shifts new-fallen snow over the landscape, it deposits it on lee slopes, building folds of windpacked snow or cornices on the crown of the slope as it passes overhead. These cornices may grow to huge dimensions, ominously overhanging the slope below. Cornices tell you that the slope below them has been loaded with wind-transported snow, perhaps five times the depth of snow that has fallen. That additional weight puts severe stress on weak bonds in the snowpack. The movement of a single skier on the slope may cause it to release. Even if the slope is stable, the cornice may release.

Avalanches at lift-served resorts today are rare, but not unheard of. There have, in fact, been several avalanche fatalities at western ski areas in recent years. Although modern avalanche control does not allow cornices to build to menacing proportions, avalanche control is still not an exact science. In the backcountry every cornice and lee slope is a potential avalanche. Approach corniced slopes in the backcountry with respect.

Because of the instability involved, the best way to avoid avalanche is through proper route selection and slope stability analysis. Nevertheless, you should know what to do in case of entrapment and burial. On a backcountry tour, if you encounter a suspect slope that must be crossed, remember these rules:

1) Cross one at a time.
2) Release your pole straps and ski safety straps, and loosen your pack straps so that poles, skis and packs may be shed in an emergency. Such equipment acts as handles for the snow to grip and pull you under.
3) While crossing, you should put your beeper on transmit, and make sure it is next to the skin and cannot be torn away. The transmit button should be taped down. A 100-foot avalanche cord attached to the waist would provide additional insurance.
4) Make sure all clothing is drawn tight, especially the collar of your jacket, so that snow will not pack into your clothing.
5) Before crossing, survey the slope for islands of safety that an avalanche would move around—patches of trees or a rock outcropping. Stay close to these islands. If you need to stop while crossing, do so only at these points. Try to cross high on the slope.
6) Avoid slopes that terminate in ravines or cliffs. You don't want to be swept into a deep gully or over a long drop.
7) If your friends cannot see the entire slope below the crossing, post an avalanche sentry at a position where he can see the slope. Had the Holcombs (see sidebar) been able to see the character of the slope below them, they might not have made their near fatal crossing.
8) If you see an avalanche bearing down upon you or experience one starting under your skis, traverse to the edge of the avalanche track if possible. Don't try to outrun the avalanche downslope.
9) If caught, try to shed your skis, poles and pack, and use vigorous swimming motions to stay on the surface.
10) If pulled under, try to clear an air pocket in front of your face as you feel the avalanche slow. Inhale several times getting some extra breath, then thrust one arm upward. Several skiers have been rescued quickly because a hand projected above the surface.

Practice search technique for a buried victim *before* you go on your backcountry tour or trek. Your intent is to recover a victim *within four minutes* even though a few lucky skiers have survived a half hour; fewer have survived longer.

HYPOTHERMIA, FROSTBITE AND FIRST AID

The other chief dangers in backcountry skiing are frostbite and hypothermia.

In hypothermia the body's vital systems begin to shut down because the core temperature lowers. It manifests itself in early stages as extreme cold discomfort and impaired judgment. There is intense shivering, fatigue and a feeling of numbing cold. The victim suffers an inability to care for himself; he has difficulty thinking clearly and coping generally.

The mildly hypothermic victim must be warmed immediately. He or she should be gotten out of the wind and cold, wet clothes replaced with dry clothes. The person should be warmed with hot drinks and hot water bottles. Use any available containers. If the victim has slipped into advanced stages of hypothermia, he will be unable to warm himself.

The classic treatment for hypother-

Jim Holcomb and his wife E.J. had been skiing mid-April corn snow near their home. They decided to take a three-day tour with their friend Garrett to the high country.

Near the tree line, they found that the snow had not corned up on the south slopes, but had stayed hard, so hard that they could not drive a ski tip into the surface easily. Because a fall on that kind of snow meant a long slide, they were forced onto a rocky ridge where they had to walk. Late afternoon they dug a snowcave in the dense wind crust of a northerly exposure.

On the second morning they were traversing across steep wind crust slopes and through scattered white bark pine.

"There was a little gully, about fifty to sixty feet across. It didn't look bad," said Jim.

"To go up would mean gaining a lot of vertical, then a nasty knife edge and a cornice. We figured we couldn't get over the cornice," said E.J. "Instead, we decided to ski across one at a time and be real careful."

Garrett skied across the gully into a little knot of trees. While E.J. was skiing across, she caught her binding in the hard snow, flipped and skidded down the slope into a tree well. "I was cursing away, beginning to take my skis off to right myself when it happened."

"I was in the middle of the gully. It sounded like a sonic boom," said Jim. "The snow cracked across into the trees, the crack going down six feet. I looked around. Everything was moving. I thought, oh my God, I'm going to die. I said swim, let's swim. Suddenly I was down. Even though all my pack straps were loose and my waistbelt undone, there was no time to get out of the pack. I went maybe a thousand feet, getting worked over, finally being pushed to the side where I grabbed a tree."

In the tree well, E.J. looked up and saw the whole thing happen. "I locked my hands around the tree. A big block smashed into my arm. The tree was shaking, branches snapping. It was like being in a wind tunnel, my feet straight out while things were rushing past me. It was insane. I was thinking this is it, I'm a goner."

Garrett was knocked down, washed over a little knoll, then pushed safely to the side.

The avalanche lasted fifteen to twenty seconds. The slope had fractured into big blocks, chunks the size of pianos and Volkswagens. The avalanche ran the full length of the track, a half mile to the bottom. All three skiers were lucky to be caught near the starting point or the crown of the avalanche. Jim was fortunate on three counts. The nature of the snow—dense slab—allowed his vigorous movements to keep him rafting along on top of the snow instead of being pulled under. He was able to grab a tree. Another ten feet and he would have been swept over a short cliff and buried beneath blocks of snow that would have taken, in Jim's words, a crane to remove.

mia—immersing the hypothermic victim in warm water—is rarely available in the backcountry. Rescuers will have to do what they can to rewarm the victim's core areas—head, neck, torso and groin. This includes the gentle application of hot water bottles and packs and the use of their own body heat.

The deeply hypothermic victim is a severe medical case. Too much heat can return warm blood to a "cold heart" causing it to fibrillate and the victim to die of cardiac arrest. Essentially, it is best to keep this person in "cold storage," protecting him from further cold exposure, gently adding heat as indicated until evacuation can be effected.

Frostbite is the actual freezing of fluids in the body's cells—usually in fingers, toes, ear, nose—in those peripheral areas where circulation is poorest. Its first symptoms are familiar to most people who live in snow environments. The tissue is blanched and bloodless at first. Loss of feeling and numbness in hands and feet call for immediate efforts at rewarming. After stopping and/or getting out of the weather, stimulate the affected area by rubbing and heat applications. The idea is to get warm blood circulating through the affected tissue.

The tissue is frozen in advanced frostbite—it is cold and hard. Advanced frostbite calls for rapid rewarming by immersion in warm water. However, the use of the affected tissues after thawing will cause further damage. An advanced frostbite victim who has been "thawed" must be evacuated. One option is to allow the victim to ski out "frozen," rewarming the tissues when a safe environment has been reached.

Removing or adding clothing layers in timely fashion should preclude frostbite and hypothermia.

If you're skiing above 8,000 feet, altitude sickness can also be a problem. As we stated in Chapter 5, altitude sickness symptoms vary; persistent headaches and shortness of breath are typical. Nausea and a general unease or restlessness are also indicative. The solution is simple— get the person to a lower elevation. With rest, recovery is rapid. To avoid altitude sickness, ascend slowly, allowing the body to acclimate—an easy rule to break while on skis. (See Chapter 5 for further discussion.)

The most common medical problems on a high mountain ski tour or long trek are blistering feet and skin exposure to sun, wind and cold. Rich creams keep hands from cracking. Generous dollops of the highest rating sunscreens and liberal use of chapsticks protect exposed skin and lips. With these measures you'll come off a haute route bronzed rather than looking like the skin of a baked apple.

The toughest feet can suffer blisters on a long haute route. To prevent blisters, everyone should tape or place patches of adhesive knit on heels and bony prominences before booting up. Every skier should have a blister kit consisting of patches of knit, moleskin, molefoam and gel, as well as waterproof athletic tape, a topical antibiotic like Neosporin and a combination knife that includes scissors and tweezers, for trimming and applying bandages. In addition, everyone should carry aspirin, a minor assortment of Band-Aids, roller and triangular bandages and an elastic knee brace of appropriate size. Each tour member should be schooled in first aid.

Giardia, a microscopic organism that inhabits wilderness water, can raise more havoc with your digestive tract than Montezuma's Revenge. We've seen friends get it from drinking overflow water beneath the snow cover on frozen Alpine lakes.

With the exception of snow, boil all water to ensure against giardia.

For the sake of safety, carry a complete repair kit into the far backcountry. Losing your skis and poles in the far backcountry is akin to being marooned on an island in an ocean. Each group should carry one extra pair of skis and poles or the materials and tools to repair damaged equipment. A comprehensive repair kit for the party will contain:

1) Tools: A combination tool that has pliers, crescent wrench and screwdrivers, or the individual tools themselves; a small needle-nosed vise grip and punch for binding removal and replacement;
2) Spare Parts: cross-country tour skiers should carry both left and right 3-pin

binding plates, bails and screws; Alpine tourers should carry binding parts appropriate for the type of binding they have. Bring an emergency ski tip, pole basket and straps, as well as pack straps and buckles;

3) Repair paraphernalia: strapping tape, picture hanging wire, nylon cord, pole splint, nylon patch, superglue and steel wool.

In addition to the group kit, a few repair/replacement items (i.e., extra binding bails, pack straps, head lamp batteries and bulbs) and a sewing kit should be carried by each tour member. A group kit carried by someone at the bottom of the crest does not help the skier near the top who just broke a binding bail.

Apart from avalanche, the biggest concern while touring the backcountry is an injury or sickness that renders a skier unable to continue. Evacuation of a trail mate in the winter backcountry is extremely difficult. In that event you will either have to sled the skier out, or bring in a helicopter. Remember—skidding an injured skier out on a jury-rig sled can be traumatic for the victim and trying for the rescuers. Yet the alternative of dragging a backcountry sled with you on tour is often not a very satisfactory option either.

Most Forest Service districts and all wilderness area management require skiers to acquire a permit before their tour. That requirement is primarily a safety measure. The backcountry safety information provided here should be reinforced with more comprehensive instruction in the mountains. Intensive snow safety courses conducted in avalanche country are offered by the U.S. Forest Service, as well as by a few private organizations—the best known of which is the American Avalanche Institute of Wilson, Wyoming. The AAI conducts several two- and three-day intensive backcountry ski courses each season in avalanche education and protection. Courses are led by the most noted experts in the country.

Professional Ski Instructor of America ski schools specializing in backcountry skiing are not yet generally available. However, some instruction in backcountry technique may be available through existing Alpine and track schools, especially those that offer backcountry day tours.

Instruction that covers all facets of backcountry skiing—ski techniques, snow camping, equipment, food and clothing and safety—is available only through backcountry ski outfitters. In the end, such outfitters may be the best choice. You can learn while on an actual guided tour.

BACKCOUNTRY SKIING EQUIPMENT

Terrain, snow and your skiing objectives dictate the choice of ski equipment in the backcountry. In addition to skis, poles and boots, light backpacks are commonly used by many day tourers. The far backcountry skier requires specific equipment and clothing for overnight camping in snow.

If you're staying in flat valleys or rolling terrain, and avoiding descents, you can use the light touring skis and shoes used for groomed trail touring. But if the snow is deep powder, or is glazed, or if you are wearing a backpack bigger than a day pack, or if you are a large individual (over 180 pounds), light touring equipment simply does not provide enough support for backcountry touring in low terrain. You will need a

Backcountry sleds save one from heavy backpack loads and are a safety hedge in the event of an accident. They are very useful on treks that follow flat valleys or open country, and on firm snow, but are much less manageable in Alpine terrain and deep snow. *(Bob Jonas)*

heavier, wider ski and a higher, stiffer boot.

If you also want to tour in the mountains, you will need heavier gear—including a ski with a metal edge to help hold you on glazed snow or steep slopes. Therefore, for general backcountry touring, you should select an edged cross-country downhill ski (also called a mountaineering or telemark ski). To avoid waxing for the changing conditions of the backcountry, choose a waxless model with a firm tour boot suitable for making easy turns.

If you're primarily interested in downhill backcountry skiing, you have two choices: a cross-country downhill or Alpine tour system.

The cross-country downhill skier wears a firm leather boot for downhill

skiing support. Many choose a double boot. You can choose the same waxless edged downhill ski used for touring, or waxable models that have less camber and perform better in downhill skiing.

The Alpine touring system features a light weight plastic boot and a release binding that detaches at the heel for touring, and reattaches for the downhill descent. The binding provides the same rigid support as the fixed Alpine downhill binding. The Alpine touring ski is typically short in length. Otherwise, it's similar in width, weight and character to the Alpine downhill ski.

Alpine touring, practically unknown in this country, has been practiced for years in Europe. In the Alps snow conditions are more varied than snow conditions in the drier inland Rockies. In the Alps, the terrain is very steep. Steep terrain with mixed snow conditions calls for stable, supportive downhill equipment. Some areas in the high Alps are accessible by tram or chairlift. Lift access reduces the overland mileage you have to ski, making the heavy rigid Alpine touring system perfect for the comparatively short touring distances along Alpine crests.

American ski touring is different. In the West, there are the dramatic Alpine crests, but those crests are typically miles from the nearest road or lift-serviced mountain. Elsewhere, vast forests, low round mountains, and rolling terrain offer both excellent downhill and tour skiing. It's not surprising that most Americans choose a cross-country system.

Bob Rosso, a total skier who for twelve years has owned a shop specializing in mountain sports, makes the following observation on the choice of backcountry downhill equipment:

"There is a dramatic difference in

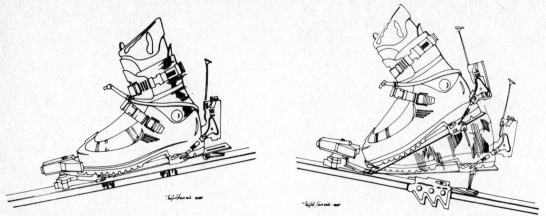

The Alpine tour system utilizes a rigid light-weight plastic boot and Alpine style binding that locks the heel for the descent (left). For the ascent, the heel is released and the toe moves to a pivot position on a hinge. A heel lift can be sprung into place to serve for ascending steep slopes, thus preventing achilles tendon and calf muscle fatigue. A detachable ski crampon helps to hold the ski firm on very hard snow surfaces.

skiing Alpine touring gear as opposed to free-heel cross-country downhill gear. Alpine touring gear is extremely mechanical because you have to have a release mechanism. It's also heavy."

Rosso is quick to point out the problems of cross-country downhill, too. "Big guys have a hard time with this gear because the skis are too narrow and unstable. And the three-pin binding, which is wider than the ski, can hook on the snow during a sharp turn when skiing on packed conditions or firm surfaces.

"The Alpine touring system is for the downhill skier who wants to hike up a ridge and ski down a slope, period. Up top, on the steep and in a variety of snow conditions Alpine touring gear really gives you a lot more power and control to ski the terrain. But if you want to enjoy the roving aspect of skiing the backcountry, you should go free heel."

Co-author Bob Jonas and four friends chose an Alpine touring system for a forty-one-day, 150-mile trek through Alaska's Wrangell Mountain range. They knew they would need the stability of Alpine equipment for descents down three big mountains along the all glacier route. They knew snow conditions could be difficult high in the mountains. They were carrying heavy packs and each towing a sled, more reasons for the stability of Alpine touring gear. They also knew that the long tours between descents—and the ascents— would be easier on a cross-country system. On a climb or tour, the three-pin stride, with the foot flexing at the ball, is a more natural, easy motion.

They opted on the side of safety in choosing an Alpine system for a long trek in remote country. Still, at the end of the trail the opinions were divided about the ski system of choice. Co-author Seth Masia, on the other hand, chose three-pins and telemark skis for a five-day trip in the Alps. The long climbs went quickly on the light gear, but steep descents on hard glacial snow proved difficult.

The Alpine touring ski has very little camber compared to most cross-country downhill skis. That means it does not tour well; the skier slips backward on the slightest incline. You have to keep ski skins on, or wax heavily, to prevent slipping. This is also the problem with high performance cross-country downhill skis—they lack touring performance.

Because backcountry skiers encounter a variety of snow conditions, and because speed is relatively unimportant, both cross-country and Alpine tour skis are softer in the tip and have a uniform flex, compared to Alpine downhill skis. If you are fortunate enough to discover a deep powder mecca through the season

Skiers apply an imperative piece of equipment for the backcountry downhill skier: climbing skins. *(Bob Jonas)*

you may want an even softer ski. Safety or runaway straps for powder skiing are highly advisable. Digging for a submerged ski that has released from your foot can be both exhausting and fruitless. And losing a ski in a remote locale can be dangerous.

There should be an interesting future in backcountry ski equipment. The cross-country or Alpine tour option will likely always exist, though developments may tip the scale to one choice. A few manufacturers are producing Alpine tour skis that are extremely light. For free-heel skiers who want the stability and downhill performance of an Alpine ski, that's good news. But they are still far from ideal for touring. Many free-heel skis are now being made shorter and wider—more like Alpine touring skis. These may prove ideal.

For both Alpine and cross-country downhill skiers in the backcountry, synthetic climbing skins are an imperative. Skins enable you to ascend slopes without having to resort to switchback climbing.

Another important quality of most skins is that you can safely descend many slopes in control with the skin attached. For anyone who is concerned about backcountry downhill control, the skin can be a blessing. Skins have also been used as a teaching aid to help skiers maintain control while learning telemark technique.

Purchase a skin that is the width and length of your skis; do not compromise with a "skinny skin," one of abbreviated length or width (width is more critical).

The ski pole favored for the backcountry is an adjustable length pole that has an Alpine style shaft and grip. The adjustable length enables the backcountry skier to lengthen the pole for touring or shorten it for downhill skiing. And when making a long traverse on a steep

A skier makes a steep ascent avoiding a more time-consuming switchback climb. *(Bob Jonas)*

slope, the skier can shorten the uphill pole while keeping the downhill pole long.

The Alpine style grip is more secure for downhill skiing and provides a convenient platform and finger grip indentations for climbing. Some manufacturers provide a self-arrest grip that has a hook for use in arresting oneself when skidding down a steep slope.

The pole shaft should be made of modern anodized aluminum. *Do not* take fiberglass or other synthetic shafted poles into the far backcountry. They are more likely to break. The poles should mate with each other to form a single long avalanche probe for use in helping to locate victims buried in avalanche debris.

There are several brands of Alpine tour bindings available. On a long trek a light binding that is strong and repairable in the field is desirable. An Alpine tour binding has a heel mechanism that releases for free-heel touring and can be locked for downhill skiing. The American-made Ramer and the French Petzl binding are the best of the lot.

Backpacks for the far backcountry should be frameless, have a number of adjustment points, side pockets or straps to carry skis and a well-padded hipbelt. Several excellent choices exist today. Make sure the pack fits well—you'll be skiing downhill with thirty to sixty pounds in your backpack's compartments, and you don't want it swinging loosely.

While snowcaves may be satisfactory

shelter for many backcountry treks, carrying a tent is often desirable, especially if you expect to find very wet snow or cold, hard snow that will be difficult or impossible to dig in. You'll find hard snow in far northern mountains and on broad glaciers.

A backpack shovel is essential for the backcountry. It can be used to dig snow shelters, make a snow camp and dig people and skis out of the snow. Two choices exist: plastic shovels and those with a hard aluminum blade. While modern polycarbonate plastics make for a durable blade, the aluminum blade is better for cutting very hard or densely compacted snow.

Warm sleeping bags are also essential. Down is warm, light and can be stuffed into a small space or sack—all important criteria for the long trail. A Gore-Tex fabric bivouac sack keeps down from getting wet in snow caves. Buy a full-length sleeping pad as well. We prefer the "Therm-a-Rest" brand air pad and an Ensolite closed-cell foam pad. The Ensolite foam provides extra insulation under the air mattress at night and is used for sitting on the snow around camp.

For the far backcountry, clothing should include a mountain suit—separate jacket and pants or bib pants. Any pair of pants should have side zips to allow for easy ventilation. Both jacket and pants, of course, must be wind and water resistant. Additonally, an expedition weight down parka with a hood is a good idea, especially in high, cold mountains. It's great for instant warmth during stops on the trail, at camps, and if you're a cold sleeper, it can add fifteen more degrees of warmth to your sleeping bag.

A baseball cap or, better, a cap with a bill front and back keeps the sun from your eyes and from blistering your neck. Take three pairs of hand covers: lightweight leather gloves for hot days (they can also be used to handle hot pots at night), insulated Gore-Tex gloves for mid- and cold ranges, mittens or heavier gloves plus an overmitt of Gore-Tex fabric that reaches to the elbow for brittle cold. The overmitt also serves you well during cave digging, which can be a wet affair. Carry a face mask, neck gaiter or balaclava hat for blizzard and stinging cold.

If you're skiing on cross-country downhill equipment, a double leather boot is best for the long trail. It's warmer and stays dry longer. Combined with an overbootie, the inner boot makes an excellent camp boot and will dry each night in your bag with you. A super gaiter, which fits over the entire boot, helps to keep the leather dry. The gaiter adds extra insulation for cold days, too. There are a number of Alpine tour boots available. They should be as light as possible without compromising fit or downhill skiing stability. Take extra pains to make sure they fit well. Plastic is unforgiving; your feet will look like hamburger after a long trail if the fit is poor. Try several models and makes, if available. The inner boot should be insulated and flex well without any bind or sore spots. The entire boot shell and inner boot should rocker forward comfortably for all the climbing and touring that occurs on a haute route.

The step turn used in a NASTAR race. *(Bob Jonas)*

9
Citizen Competition

Entering ski competition takes you one step further along the path of the Total Skier. It is a way to test and expand your skill and to sharpen your skiing experience.

Any recreational skier can ski race. You do not have to be affiliated with scholastic or collegiate competition, professional ski racing or the competitive organization—the United States Ski Association (USSA), the national skiing body through which young aspiring skiers ascend to national team status. Many skiing communities organize both downhill and cross-country races for their citizens (now called sports racing), and there is organized national ski competition open to all skiers. It's all part of the response to the national craze for fitness and athletic competition in every sport. The USSA, too, has a place for the citizen ski competitor, and it offers Masters races for the dedicated adult skier.

Skiing competition can be thought of as a game of speed and control. Alpine skiing events test your skill at controlling speed; cross-country track events test your ability to effect and maintain speed.

ALPINE RACING

Downhill citizen skiing events (commonly known as Alpine events) include slalom, giant slalom and, rarely, super giant slalom and downhill. The object is to negotiate a series of control gates on the slope faster than anyone else. The start and finish are electronically monitored to hundredths of a second, as that is often the margin of victory.

Each gate consists of two poles set upright in the snow between which the competitor must pass. If the poles are set in a horizontal plane—across the fall line—it is an open gate. Two poles set in a vertical plane—one below the other in the fall line—is a closed gate. Closed gate poles may also be set obliquely—in an offset closed position. Two closed gates in a row, set vertically, is termed a hairpin; three or four, a flush.

A *slalom* course takes approximately a minute to run, but length will vary. The international ski body governing ski competition, the Federation Internationale de Ski (FIS), sets specific standards. Women's slalom courses are forty-five to sixty gates in length, men's fifty-five to seventy-five. There are limitations relative to the vertical drop of the slope over which a course may be set. Slalom gates are set close to each other down the fall line. It takes approximately a second to negotiate a gate while running a course. The whole course is a continuous combination of open and closed gates, hairpins and flushes.

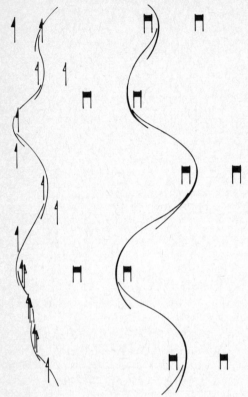

A slalom race course (left) has more gates than a giant slalom course (right), the typical citizen Alpine race course.

Because of the many gates set close together, necessitating a lot of short, tight turns, the slalom is a low-speed race course typically less than 15 mph. A competitor makes two runs in slalom, usually on two different courses. The competitor with the lowest combined time wins. The winner is usually the skier most adept at turning quickly.

The *giant slalom*—commonly known as GS—is a race course one to two-and-a-half-minutes long. The gates will vary in number but thirty to forty-five is typical. The FIS has a standard relating the number of gates to the vertical drop of a slope. A giant slalom course consists of all open and closed gates; there are no hairpins or flushes. Gates are spaced much farther apart; consequently the GS skier carries more speed than he would on a slalom course—racers may average 25 to 30 mph.

A GS gate is defined by two-pole sets—two poles bound together by a single banner (each pole of a slalom gate is flagged separately). The GS skier combines both slalom and downhill skills. Like slalom, two runs are made in GS, usually on two different courses.

The first race course you are likely to enter will be a NASTAR course—typically an easy abbreviated giant slalom course suitable to the range of skiing skills found among citizen racers. (NASTAR stands for National Standard Race.)

The terrain over which a course is set is an important consideration in ski competition. An FIS GS course is made up of rolls and transitions as it moves back and forth across the fall line, and it should be long enough to take forty to ninety seconds to complete, but a NASTAR course is likely to be set on consistent easy terrain and take 30 to 40 seconds.

Before running a tricky race course, competitors study gate combinations and terrain nuances. Their goal is to pick the fastest route or "line" down the course and to ski that line perfectly. At an Alpine race start area you will see racers, eyes closed, silently tracing with a hand in the air their memorized line of descent through the course. But an easy course requires no memorization. Gates follow each other in a simple left-right-left-right sequence.

Competitive Alpine racing is not limited to young skiers. It can be performed at all age levels. Loren Adkins, seventy-seven, began racing in his late sixties. Today he competes with great success, locally and nationally, in both cross-country and downhill skiing. He loves all sports, although Alpine skiing is his favorite.

"I couldn't do a thing on skis when I started," he says. "I was an athletic cripple. I had arthritis in both legs, a double hernia operation, a chronic bad back and failing vision. I was sixty-eight when I began my training program."

By virtue of discipline and dedication to his conditioning program, Loren has reversed his physical deterioration and vastly improved upon the norm for his age group. Medical tests show he has the bone structure of a thirty-five year old, the heart of a teenager. His resting pulse is 50.

Loren believes in vigorous, maximum effort in training and competition to attain an ultimate level of individual performance, what he calls "the very best you." When he trains, he skis nonstop on the open slopes; in the gates he is not timid. He skis hard and straight at the inside pole. "I love the spirit of competition. I'm always out to win my age class. It's important for the racing organizations to add the upper age classes. You need comparison with others in your age group. It makes racing real for the older people." He adds, "Young people love to have you out there too. They see me and they know they can still look forward to skiing when they're older."

The USSA provides the framework for masters races organized throughout its various nationwide divisions. Each year it sanctions a senior nationals that includes slalom, GS and downhill events. A competitor's start order at the nationals is based upon his or her results in divisional races throughout the season. Age categories begin at twenty-five and follow in seven-year increments to age fifty, five-year increments thereafter. At present, the upper class is seventy-five years and older. Any USSA member with a race card (acquired through a simple application process) can compete at the nationals. However the "seeding" process, based upon a competitor's results throughout the season in the divisional races, is an advantage for the best skiers.

Top seeded racers race early in the start order when the course is in optimum condition. Those who run later face a deteriorating course, which makes it difficult to finish at the top. During the season the goal, therefore, is to establish good results throughout the year in your own USSA division, which will earn you a higher seed at the nationals. Masters competition also allows one to cross over into any division and enjoy competition against new faces.

While the Senior Nationals are the ultimate goal for many serious citizen skiers, you don't have to join a club or association to race. NASTAR, a program begun by *Ski* magazine in 1968, is the largest event of its kind in the world and the only recreational ski racing program whose basis is a national standard, similar to par in golf. *Any* skier can enter NASTAR races.

The NASTAR handicap system enables family and friends anywhere in the country to compare racing times. Currently, 133 ski areas across the nation participate in the program. Each ski area has its own NASTAR schedule, ranging from one to seven races a week.

Every participating resort offers a NASTAR giant slalom course comfortable for most recreational skiers to race. There is no slalom or downhill event in

Telemark racers compete side-by-side on a NASTAR course. *(Wood River Journal)*

NASTAR. However, in response to the growing interest in free-heel skiing, NASTAR incorporated telemark racing four years ago. Competition categories exist for juniors, adults, ski clubs and families at every NASTAR race. The adult age divisions fall into ten-year increments, beginning with ages nineteen to twenty-nine and continuing to seventy years old and up.

How does the NASTAR handicap system work? At the beginning of each new ski season the nation's top racers, including touring pros, race a NASTAR course against each other. The winner becomes the National Pacesetter and is awarded a zero handicap as the fastest NASTAR racer in the country. The zero handicap is the national standard against which all NASTAR racers are measured.

The zero handicap is applied to individual ski area courses when the National Pacesetter competes against local pacesetters at regional trials. The local pacesetter is then handicapped based on how much slower he is than the National Pacesetter at the regional trials.

The local pacesetter then returns to the local course and establishes "par time" each day. Par time is the theoretical time the National Pacesetter should have raced the course. It is the local pacesetter's time minus his or her handicap.

When you race a NASTAR course, you automatically receive a handicap based on your finish time. With that handicap you're able to compare yourself with the best on the mountain and in the nation. The handicap bases make NASTAR an individual affair; you're racing against yourself and the clock to improve your handicap. Depending upon your handicap, age and sex you can win gold, silver or bronze NASTAR medals. The best handicap times in each of five NASTAR regional divisions are invited, expenses paid, to race the national finals each year at a selected area.

Another opportunity for citizen competitors to race Alpine nationally is the Equitable Family Ski challenge. Lori and Bob Sarchett won the husband/wife national cup in 1980; Chris and Bob won the father/son cup in 1982. Again, for the national level competitors, all expenses are paid. They earn their berth winning local and regional competitions that are sponsored by the Equitable Life Assurance Society.

Telemark gate racing, organized under local and regional citizens' race organizations, is also gaining in popularity today. A national championship is held annually at Crested Butte, Colorado, where telemarking began its renaissance.

All ages and sizes compete on NASTAR courses. Here, a Denver five year old speeds toward a gold medal finish. *(NASTAR/Batlin)*

A RACING FAMILY

The Sarchett family are all competitive Alpine skiers. Bob was a dedicated recreational skier who mastered the bumps (moguls)—the most serious challenge for the recreational skier. But before long, he found himself bored with bumps. "Bump skiing is a sport for twenty-two year olds," he says. "My back began to get sore." He felt he had reached a plateau as a skier and looked to racing at age thirty. "In racing there are no more plateaus," he says. "Every day I can feel myself get better. The clock shows the improvement."

Lori, his wife, began competing a little later. "I still remember that first time through a race course. Racing was hard for me to learn but it was so much fun, such a rush."

Their three boys grew up in the gates. Now Chris, the oldest, is taking a recess from competition, concentrating, ironically, on bump skiing. Jeff continues as a very serious and dedicated racer with national team aspirations. Robin, ten years younger than Chris, is an excellent technical skier. He has progressed faster than the older boys. "We don't know if he will be a serious racer—we're not pushing."

Skiing on one of the world's premier ski mountains, Mt. Baldy in Sun Valley, seven days a week, the Sarchetts confine themselves, 75 percent of the time, to one small area. There, three hours a day, they practice racing through the gates. They're not just training for a coming race. For the Sarchetts and many like them, gate skiing is a sport in itself.

ALPINE RACING TECHNIQUES

The essence of a good giant slalom run is the feeling of skis that are running on rails with little or no side slipping, as you rhythmically clip inside poles, not a millimeter off your line.

At the core of good Alpine race technique is independent leg action. The fast Alpine skier actually *skates* through the gates, moving like a cross-country track racer, speed skater or hockey player. The weight is on one ski at a time, and at the end of each turn the racer can gain speed by pushing powerfully off one ski onto the other in the racing step turn.

THE RACING STEP

The racing step turn, in its most basic form, is easy to learn. First, you must learn how to skate:

1) Start on smooth, flat terrain—a cat track is best. It should be someplace flat enough that your skis won't glide unless you pole or skate along.
2) Skate from one ski to the other, balancing yourself by using the opposite ski pole.
3) As you step off the edge of the left ski, your weight goes naturally toward the right ski. As you weight the right ski and begin to shift toward the left, the ski rolls onto its inside edge. Push off the edge onto the left ski. Skating soon becomes a smooth, rhythmic motion. The key to it is to allow the ski to roll from edge to edge.

Once you're comfortable with Alpine skating on flat terrain, move to a smooth gentle slope. A beginner slope is best, but because you'll be moving faster than most of the beginners, choose a time when you can have the run to yourself. As you ski downhill, pick up one ski, then the other—right off the snow. Then combine this with a turn. You'll find it gradually easier and easier to lift the inside ski clear of the snow.

A giant slalom racer demonstrating the racing step turn. The key element of the turn is an aggressive step onto the uphill ski from a strongly edged downhill ski.

Now you're ready to use the skate in the step turn. At the end of a turn, as you put the inside ski back down on the snow, extend the outside leg powerfully, skating forward onto the new ski (see drawing above). Then roll the new ski onto the inside edge while carving another turn. Step by step, here's a complete racing step turn sequence:

1) Just before making a turn to the left, your weight is on the right uphill ski. You've picked the left ski up off the snow;

2) Ride the right ski around to the end of the turn;

3) Push hard against the right ski by straightening the right leg. At the top of this motion, place the left ski back on the snow. This is a stepping-up motion, from right ski to left. It's the same skating motion you've been practicing, but it has the effect of moving you a couple of feet uphill;

4) You are now standing on the left ski, with the right ski off the snow. As you glide into the fall-line aiming toward the next gate, ski onto its inside edge to start carving the new turn to the right;

5) Ride the left ski around to the end of the turn, keeping your weight and body poised over that ski;

6) Skate or step up onto the right ski;

7) You are now standing on the right ski, with the left ski off the snow. Roll the right ski onto its inside edge to start a new turn to the left.

Repeat the sequence. As you grow in confidence, you'll find that you gain speed with each step. At first this will feel scary—you've always depended on turning to slow you down, to control your speed. Now, you're using the turn to speed up. But racers, after all, are in the business of going faster.

A simple exercise may help you learn to balance on one ski through the turn. Start by traversing, in a straight line, all the way across the slope. Pick the uphill ski off the snow as you glide, and hold it there until it's time to turn. When you're comfortable with that, try picking up the downhill ski, and traverse standing only on the uphill ski. That's tougher, but not too tough.

Now at an angle downslope, traverse halfway on the downhill ski, put down the uphill ski, stand on it, pick up the downhill ski—and turn! Turn standing on the uphill ski only. As you complete the turn, you'll find yourself standing on the same ski, but now it's the downhill ski. To make this exercise into a racing step turn, it's only necessary to add the skate where the change of skis has been.

Practice the skate step turn on the beginner hill until it feels natural, then try it on a smooth intermediate slope. You'll be surprised at how quickly you gain speed—but you'll also find you're turning with control at that speed. Gradually increase your speed by shortening the end of the turn. Instead of waiting for the skis to arc all the way into a traverse position, you'll skate onto the new uphill ski while the old ski is still pointing downhill, closer to the fall line. To reduce your speed, go back to completing the turn.

Now take your step turn to the race course. Watch the fastest skiers carefully, and you'll see how to time the skate between the gates. Practice in an open gate course first.

A couple of years ago co-author Seth Masia coached two beginning racers from New York who had entered a corporate NASTAR race in Vail. Ellen and Jamie were good athletes and solid intermediate skiers who had never had any race training.

They tried to run the gates with their weight on both skis. The skis skidded and skittered around the course. The top racers were finishing the course under 30 seconds while Ellen and Jamie wound up with times in the low 50s. Before the second run Seth went through the step turn exercises described above with them. That afternoon Ellen and Jamie skied the course again, this time carving and skating one ski at a time. They reduced their times to under 40 seconds and Ellen's team won a trophy. "Not only that," she told Seth later, "I used that step turn on icy snow back home and I have a lot better control now. My skis held on the ice and I'm a lot smoother and more confident."

Jamie was so delighted that she signed up for race camp and bought a pair of 205 cm slalom skis. On some days she's now faster than her teacher.

The best way to get started racing is through the assistance of understanding friends in a local racing club. Many PSIA ski schools, in response to the interest in citizen Alpine racing, offer instruction in gate skiing. If no assistance is available, ski the NASTAR course on your own. Just as descending many miles on a big challenging mountain hones your technical responses to terrain, you'll start making adjustments to the action of the course, provided you're skiing aggressively rather than sliding around the inside pole of a gate at arm's length. Only with that boldness will you master any trepidation you may have about a given course.

Another alternative is to attend a week-long ski race camp. Such camps are offered at various locales in the American West and in Europe, both midwinter and in late spring. In warm weather, these camps mix skiing with other sports such as tennis, boardsailing and mountain climbing. The camps are attended by aspiring racers. *Ski* magazine runs a directory listing of summer race camps in its spring issue each year.

Once you do begin ski racing, you can always get better. The clock shows improvement.

Loren Adkins describes his early progress in the Masters downhill this way: "First you don't even know if you can do it. When you are skiing fast, you feel anxiety—you don't know if you can finish the race. Once you have finished a few courses, you begin sorting out the technique. The last stage is refinement and fun." What is a race like? Loren describes his run at the Senior National Downhill at Whitefish, Montana, thus:

"The first part of the course was a long schuss into a corner. Looking down on the people below wasn't bad, but watching the young skiers squirt down the course and disappear, I thought, you gotta turn at that speed and make the corner? That was frightening. I just took off as if training, but really anchored myself over the skis on the corner. The electronic gun clocked me at fifty-one miles per hour.

"After the corner I was tired and there was only one place to relax. Of course, you're still going like hell. Then they turned you into the waterfalls and it really is a series of waterfalls—steep and icy. They put in an extra gate just before the first waterfall for the old folks. Here you are, diving off the first waterfall in a near freefall, and then you had to cut across the mountain at this terrific speed. The next waterfall you again are diving out into space, literally flying. You couldn't even check yourself, you couldn't slow down, you didn't dare." [A racer "checks" his speed by making extra turns between gates or holding onto a turn in a speed checking slide on the ski edges—not always a safe maneuver at high speed—rather than letting his skis glide free off the edges.]

"At the bottom were three compression rolls. The rolls literally beat you, and here I was completely worn out from fighting the waterfalls. You hit the first one fast, banging down on those skis. The next roll throws you into the air and you wonder what position you will be in when you come down. Then you hit the third roll."

Loren finished the race upright and, at age seventy-seven, won his age class.

CROSS-COUNTRY TRACK RACING

Cross-country track competition, like Alpine competition, requires technical finesse. But unlike Alpine skiing, it demands the power, strength and endurance necessary to sprint miles at a time if one is to keep close to the leaders. Typical citizen race distances are ten, fifteen and twenty-five kilometers. Marathon racing, fifty kilometers and longer, is also popular.

Unlike Alpine racing, cross-country track racing requires the strength and endurance to sprint for miles at a time. *(John Plummer)*

Organized cross-country racing for citizens takes place primarily at the local level. You'll find citizen races held wherever cross-country is popular—many a ski town will even host a winter-long racing series to crown a local cross-country champion. Categories are established by age in increments of ten years, in addition to an open class. Competitors range from tots to oldsters. The USSA has a Master's program for serious citizen racers. It too is organized into different age groups, in increments of five years. As in Alpine racing, the USSA sponsors a national championship.

The very popular "Great American

Ski Chase," a series of marathons held at eight locations across the country, is open to all cross-country skiers. The distances range from fifty kilometers (thirty miles) to eighty kilometers (forty-nine miles). To win the age class title for the season, a citizen must accumulate points in at least three races. The combined finishes of a skier's three best races determine the age class champions for each age classification. The classic event in the series is the American Bierkebeiner at Telemark, Wisconsin. The midwinter "Bierkie" is to cross-country skiing what the Boston Marathon is to running. The Bierkie attracts up to 10,000 skiers, most of whom are citizens following behind the elite racers of the world.

The Bierkie existed before the Chase was established. In addition to being part of the Chase, it is one of ten races that make up the World Loppet series, an international marathon competition for citizens and national team racers.

Many citizen cross-country track racers now ski marathons. Marathons are not so intimidating as the distances may lead one to believe. The smooth, even gliding motion on flats and downhills make cross-country marathons much easier than road-running marathons. A citizen racer can settle into a comfortable pace and even tour a marathon course rather than race.

Marathon courses often wind through fields, over hills, through woodland copses and deep evergreen forests; across streams and frozen lakes and through valleys. High prominences often provide commanding views of the countryside and colorful villages. The pace can be fun; uphills mean a downhill will follow. It is a mixture of rhythm and technique.

In Europe, where 10,000 skiers start in a typical marathon, the atmosphere is festive. As the course winds through villages, thousands of people cheer and pat the racers as they pass. It is not uncommon to see skiers wearing race bibs enjoying a glass of wine with the locals at a wayside table before they continue.

The American Bierkebeiner, held annually in Cable, Wisconsin. Thousands of skiers turn out for the great ski marathons. *(Bierkebeiner Staff Photo)*

The marathons have more difficult moments, too: a blizzard can obliterate the tracks, making skiing difficult. The tip of the nose, cheekbones, earlobes and fingertips can become frostbitten if temperatures plummet. Icy tracks can make for some exciting downhills—and plenty of crashes. Traditionally, finishing racers warm themselves with a hot blueberry soup and a hot tub or sauna.

If weather threatens on race day, skiers often carry a light backpack that contains a wax kit for changing snow conditions, an anorak, face mask and warm gloves. Racers will use a light waistbelt pack for their waxing essentials. They depend upon the friendly feed station volunteers and course patrols to watch them during foul weather and offer protective clothing if needed.

On the course, the top skiers share the lead at different points in the race because the lead in cross-country is a disadvantage. The leader not only breaks the wind as in bicycle racing, but also smoothes the track to the advantage of those who follow. Often, a long race is won in the last 100 yards, when the top skiers sprint to the finish.

Another, different, cross-country race is the *biathlon.* The biathlon combines track racing with target shooting. The skier carries a .22 rifle over the typical ten kilometer distance, and must stop at targets placed along the way, shooting for accuracy. The winner is the competitor with the best combined skiing time and target score.

CROSS-COUNTRY TRACK TRAINING AND TECHNIQUES

For the top quarter of the field of skiers, fifteen kilometer races are essentially sprints from start to finish. That is becoming more and more the case for twenty-five kilometers as well. Because of that, the first goal in track racing is to build strength. Without proper conditioning you simply cannot keep pace with the front of the pack, regardless of your technique. When you get tired on a course your technique suffers. You start hanging on your poles, hunching down on every kick. With a weaker kick, you may slip on the hills, as well. If you become tired in a race, back off, and try to concentrate on smooth technique at a slower pace. Very likely you'll start feeling a second surge of energy and can make another charge with better tempo. That's often the problem in the first place—poor tempo.

How much do cross-country track skiers train? Serious citizen racers dryland train all summer and autumn. Toward the end of the dry-land period they concentrate on more ski specific activities. Of these, roller skiing is the most important (see Chapter 5). During the winter race season they hope to be peaking and train less. Some skiers train twenty-six miles a day, five days a week. But a half hour each day on the track is a good workout for the citizen racer.

Once the diagonal stride and skate techniques are mastered, they are fine-tuned for speed. Whether striding or skating, you need precise push-off and poling to maximize power in cross-country racing. Maximum glide on the very narrow unedged race ski requires perfect balance. In fact, cross-country racing can be excellent training for your Alpine gate skiing.

Increasingly, cross-country racing is becoming a "skate" race, as more and more citizen racers follow the lead of the World Cup skiers and skate an entire course, eschewing diagonal stride technique entirely. That means transitions between techniques are less important. If you have trouble balancing while skating during a race, you may be lifting your leg too high after your push-off from the skating ski. Keep the unweighted ski low as you swing it forward into the glide. That will help give you better balance and better momentum. The leg pendulums forward better when the ski is swung low, close to the ground. Lifting the leg high during recovery also results in the tendency to skate wide, creating another balance problem.

Because track competition has become a glide race with the acceptance of skating, improved performance means improving your power technique—you need more push for a longer glide. Work on your double pole and on the actual kick or skate off the ski. Here are a few tips to improve your double-poling:

1) Extend your body forward far enough that your weight is on the poles and off your heels;
2) Compress the entire upper body, so that the torso is parallel to the ground;
3) Complete the follow-through with the arms, extending them well to the rear.

The more you double-pole in a race, the faster you will ski. If you V-1 skate, learn how to V-2 skate or double-pole with *every* step down of the skated ski. Be careful not to favor your power side in the V-1 skate. Practice double-poling on both sides.

In skating, the push or kick off the skate ski should be closely timed with the double pole movements for best glide. Don't push off your skate ski until your arms have completely passed your torso. In other words, keep the glide ski flat and

Whether striding or skating, one needs perfect pole/kick timing and superior balance to finish high in cross-country track races. *(Wood River Journal)*

moving all the way through the double pole before rolling it on the inside edge for the kick. The less skilled have a habit of putting the glide ski down and then skating immediately.

Work on your timing on the hills, too. To keep your momentum and tempo on a hill, shorten your glide a bit. If you wait too long to roll the skate ski onto its edge and kick, you will come to a stop and you'll have to resort to the herringbone earlier than necessary.

The skate is the most powerful movement in track racing. Continual skating without swinging the body up for pole plants is even faster than skating with poles. Top racers are now skating on downhill sections of a course, remaining low like the ice skater on a speed oval. They use their poles only for balance.

If you are a citizen racer, you may want to try the new developments in track racing. But go slow. Start with a very easy V skate. Then experiment with double-poling on each side. The PSIA ski schools are a best bet to get the technical pointers for track racing. Then enter every citizen cross-country race that you can. You will learn how to pace yourself and pick up technique refinements by following the good skiers.

The international rules that govern all ski racing dictate that a cross-country course must be approximately one-third flat, one-third uphill and one-third downhill. You must know both yourself and the course: is skating or double-poling with the skis parallel in the track the more effective technique for you to enhance speed? Do you dare hold the tuck on that bad downhill corner, or should you wedge to control your speed? Should you start now for the finish or let the skier in front of you break the new snow on the track and shelter you from the wind a bit longer as you draft behind him? On a course with many hills should you go for striding skis and grip wax or forget about grip wax altogether and skate the entire course on skating skis?

Wax is both bane and glory for all skiers, but especially for cross-country skiers. The Alpine skier waxes for glide only. Before skating was introduced the cross-country skier had to wax for both glide and kick. The skier's waxing life is simplified now with skating. While skating, the ski edge controls the push-off, eliminating the need for a grip wax. Still, proper waxing wins races. Between two racers of nearly equal skill and strength,

the skier with the better waxed skis will emerge the winner.

Cross-country racer Mark Pearson says, "A good race derives from the perfect wax; it's good uphill and down. Your skis feel free, as if you're skiing on air." If waxing is an enigma, it is also an alibi. Ski racers have more excuses for poor performance than any other athletes. They have bad skis, broken poles, bad falls, bad days. But wax takes most of the blame. It's always a safe scapegoat.

WAXING CROSS-COUNTRY SKIS

A properly waxed ski is a joy, delivering optimum glide and consistent kick; a poorly waxed ski will slow you down, and can be worse than having no wax at all. You must choose a wax or blend of waxes carefully to match the day's snow and weather conditions.

All ski wax companies make special cross-country waxes and klisters, marking them according to a color code for appropriate snow temperatures. Warm colors (yellow, red, violet), or soft waxes, work in warm temperatures; cool colors (blue, green), or hard waxes, work in cold temperatures. There are important variations in the temperature ranges used by each wax company, so it's important to follow the waxing charts published by these firms. But in general, they tend to follow the pattern outlined in the accompanying chart.

The best way to learn waxing is to buy a complete kit of waxes from one company, read the manual that comes with it, then experiment until you find what combinations work best for you. The performance of your wax depends to some extent on the ski base material, stiffness of your own skis and the power

Generic Cross-Country Grip Wax Chart

Snow Temperature	New Snow (fallen since sunset)	Old, settled snow (one day or older)
Below 10° F	Special green, black or polar wax	Special green, black or polar wax
5 to 18° F	Green or special green	Green or special green
14 to 30° F	Green	Blue
30 to 32° F	Blue	Violet
32 to 34° F	Violet	Violet
Above 34°	Yellow	Violet klister
Above 37°	Red or yellow klister	Red or yellow klister

of your own kick, so you may have to modify the waxmaker's recommendations slightly.

WAXING FOR GLIDE AND GRIP

Skis used for traditional kick-and-glide striding need to be waxed for grip in the pocket beneath the foot so you won't slip while kicking. Think of this *kick wax* as a stickier blend of waxes. It is "soft" and may be applied a bit rough so that snow crystals readily penetrate the wax, slowing the skier or holding the kick firmly. Many high-performance skis have waxing marks visible through the clear plastic base to help you judge where to apply the kicker wax.

For the tip and tail zone of the same ski, you want a "hard" blend of waxes, smoothly polished so that snow crystals don't readily penetrate and the ski slides easily during the glide phase. This is the *glide wax.*

Skating skis are waxed for glide only and along the entire base because the kick is off the inside edge of the ski. This is another reason why skating is faster. Part of skating's popularity is that it eliminates the two-wax problem.

Wax manufacturers are responding to the surging interest in skating by making more durable glide waxes, especially for skating. And the competitors have introduced the technique of *rilling*—cutting fine grooves along the length of the ski base to improve glide.

The theory behind rilling is that fine grooves in the base help relieve minute amounts of surface suction that can develop between the ski base and the film of water on which the ski glides. Rills provide channels through which air enters and excess water escapes.

While rilling can significantly improve performance in wet snow, its value in cold, dry snow is still questionable. Some experts recommend a finer rilling pattern when snow is cold and dry, but some prefer a smooth base.

WAX APPLICATION

Working indoors, thoroughly clean the ski base with a solvent especially made for the purpose. Use a Fibertex or

Scotchbrite pad to remove burrs and align base fibers.

Choose your wax or wax blend according to experience and manufacturer recommendations. Use a waxing iron to melt the wax, drip it onto the length of the ski, then iron it smooth. A clothing iron set to the cool or wool setting works fine. Do not let the iron cause the wax to smoke at any time.

Allow the skis to cool to room temperature to ensure good penetration of the wax into the base. After cooling, working from tip to tail, scrape the wax smooth with a rigid Plexiglas scraper. For cold conditions, leave a very thin, hard layer (you shouldn't be able to roll up any wax when drawing your thumbnail over the base); leave a slightly thicker layer for wet snow.

If you rilled your base during the base prep stage, now is the time to use a nylon-bristle brush to clean the remaining wax out of the tiny rill grooves. Clean the main ski groove too. Wax left in the grooves can pick up fine dust on the track and slow the skis.

Keep the sidewalls of the ski clean, too. In fact, because skating involves a considerable sidewall-to-snow contact, especially the inside wall, they should be waxed with the same glider as you use on the base.

All waxing paraphernalia, including irons and rilling tools, can be purchased in any cross-country ski shop.

Glide waxing for Alpine skis is the same general technique as used for cross-country skating. There are no grip waxes in Alpine skiing.

As a cross-country course twists through the countryside it is exposed variably to the elements and sun. On a marathon course, snow conditions often change constantly. Waxing becomes a science.

The night before the race, a drama begins and continues into the predawn hours and through the day. Skiers and coaches secreted in basements or private corners are at their workbenches, waxing their skis. Armed with thermometers, they take the temperature of the snow outside. Hot waxes drip from irons onto skis, and are smoothed to the base. Later the skis are cooled, their newly waxed bases scraped thin and rubbed or corked to a sheen. Out in the lights of the street, one-footed skiers test the formula. Layers may be applied successively, scraped and smoothed to meet several snow conditions. Binders may be used to improve wax durability in granular snow conditions. And every expert waxer guards his secrets jealously while trying to figure out what the other waxers are using.

Morning brings either sighs of relief when snow conditions hold, or curses for new-fallen snow. Yet, even when wax is running sweet, the skier can bump into powder snow in the tracks, borne by the wind, or slip on a hill as temperatures spiral upward on a south-facing slope. When the conditions are varied, the track side is dotted with skiers scraping or waxing—especially the striders who use both grip and glide wax. At the finish, everyone may have a waxing complaint; at other times, the snow is so uniform, everyone is smiling.

Within the two worlds of Alpine and track racing, every recreational skier can find a niche to match his or her competitive spirit. Citizen racing is fun and rewarding. And it will help to refine your skiing skills, paving the path to becoming a Total Skier.

Notes

It is very difficult to wax for transitional snow—snow that is around 32 degrees Fahrenheit. Check manufacturer's recommendations carefully. Transitional snow is such a twilight zone that it can be practically impossible to find the right wax, and top racers have been known to choose a waxless ski in these conditions. High-performance skiing is possible on a waxless ski—just wax the tip and tail with a glider wax and let the kicker pattern function in place of the kick wax.

Snow that has melted and refrozen—crusty snow, ice and slush—requires special blue, purple, red or silver klisters. Check manufacturer's recommendations. Be careful using klister. If you use too much you'll never get your skis to glide forward—it's like being stuck on flypaper. Klister is gluey and messy. Keep it in its toothpaste-tube-type container, wrapped in plastic bags, to keep it from getting on everything else in your pack or wax kit.

Marc Girardelli of Luxembourg, overall World Cup winner for 1985 and 1986, in the Aspen, Colorado, Giant Slalom. Girardelli is beginning a step turn. Note that his weight is firmly on his downhill ski, and he is beginning to step uphill with his uphill ski, preparatory to making his next turn. *(Aspen Skiing Company/Kennedy)*

10
World Cup Skiing

Co-author Seth Masia writes: I'll never forget watching my first World Cup race. It was a downhill at Lake Placid in 1979, and because I was taking pictures I was allowed to stand close to the course—close enough to feel the wind of passage as racers screamed by.

And scream is an accurate description; 80 mph seems fast enough in a car, or on a motorcycle, but imagine going that fast with your feet on the ground. The noise the racers made tearing the air was a kind of fluttering whistle. I'd picked my spot at the top of the steep drop called Niagara. When the first racer—American Andy Mill—came through and sailed over the lip, my stomach dropped. So did Mill's. "Holy hell," said Mill, quietly. But he said it in the split second he passed, airborne, and I heard him over the weird wind-scream as if we were seated side-by-side in an open sports car.

World Cup racing is the most exciting spectator sport in the world, because every racer, on every run, is always on the thin edge of control. Danger is not the attraction. Modern ski racing, even the high-speed downhill, is no more dangerous than college football or show jumping. The fascination is in the concentration the sport demands, the skill achieved and the balance a racer finds between smoothly disciplined form and abandoned flailing speed.

There have been classic confrontations. Even nonskiers remember, in awe, Franz Klammer's impetuous dash to win the downhill gold medal at the 1976 Innsbruck Olympics. It was a marvelous gamble. Klammer was out of balance and out of control much of the way down course, and managed to finish only through main strength, reaction time and courage. But unless you follow ski racing regularly, you probably don't remember why he needed to gamble: it was

U.S. downhiller Holly Flanders, skiing to victory in the U.S. National Alpine championships at Vail. Holly has just cleared a jump at about 50 mph, and while she holds her aerodynamic tuck, is extending her legs to absorb the shock of landing. Note the balanced, stable position. *(Tom Lippert)*

to overtake the Swiss master Bernhard Russi, possibly the smoothest and most polished downhill skier ever. Russi had just cruised the course faultlessly, not an inch off his line, not a finger out of place. In full control all the way down, Russi had made not one mistake, and his time looked unassailable. If Klammer was going to overtake Russi, he had to break all the rules.

Every racer, in every race, has to make some such decision: shall I play it safe, and finish, or risk a fall to gain a tiny advantage? In top-level competition, where the difference between first and seventh may be measured in hundredths of a second, racers typically gamble. America's first great male racer, Coloradan Buddy Werner, said there are only two places in a race—first and last. It takes intestinal fortitude to make that gamble day after day in a racing season that stretches from August to March. Most ski racers would rather win the World Cup than an Olympic medal. The reason is simple: the World Cup is a measure of consistently excellent performance over an entire season, while an Olympic medal is based on a single race. There have been Olympic gold medal winners who never won another world-class race. But to win the World Cup you have to be more than lucky: you have to be the strongest skier in the world, that year.

That's a simple statement, but it masks a complex schedule and a Byzantine scoring system, purportedly set up to favor multitalented skiers. The Alpine World Cup rules currently call for five different types of events: slalom, giant slalom, super giant slalom, downhill and parallel slalom. Each race is worth 25 points to the winner, 20 points to the runner-up, 15 to the third-place finisher and so on down to one point for 15th place. In addition, there are combined events, in which a racer's combined finishes in two real races are added up on paper for additional points. The overall World Cup goes to the high point-winner for the year. But it's more complex than that.

Ski racing is not an easy sport to watch. The action is so fast that the untrained eye will detect differences between runs only on slow motion replays. And the margins of victory are so slender that invisible differences in line and technique can produce brilliant wins or crushing defeats. You can't see the entire course from a single standpoint, so it's most revealing to watch the race on TV.

Downhill is the easiest event to follow on television, because it's a simple one-run high-speed dash. World Cup rules require a men's downhill to fall at least 800 meters—about 2,600 feet—from start to finish, and it may be significantly longer. Most courses are two to two-and-a-half miles in length. The best racers run a typical downhill course in about 2 minutes, averaging 60 mph and skiing the steepest, straightest parts at over 80 mph.

The control gates on a downhill course were originally set only to mark the route down the mountain. During the early 1960s, however, downhill became so dangerous that officials were ordered to control speeds. Today, as part of that effort, many courses are set with artificial S-turns marked out on the steeper, faster parts, comparable to the chicane that may be placed on an auto racing straightaway to slow the cars down before nearing the pit entrance.

Success in downhill demands two quite different skills: gliding and turning. A good glider, like Bill Johnson,

America's first male Olympic gold medalist in 1984, maintains a tight, highly aerodynamic tuck and allows his skis to ride "loose" and flat on the snow. He builds up speed rapidly on straights, carries it well across flat sections, and is especially fast in softer snow. If he can also turn without losing speed, he'll win often.

Skiers who can carve fast, clean turns are said to be good technical skiers. In a fast turn, the skier must break out of his tuck position in order to edge and steer his skis accurately. Watch the skis

Phil Mahre skiing the slalom.

carefully: if they throw up a rooster-tail of snow, they may be skidding sideways; that scrubs off speed. When everything is working right, the ski rounds the turn tracking true, every inch of the steel edge passing through the same groove in the snow.

A good tuck reduces to a minimum the skier's frontal area. Over the years downhillers have refined the tuck by practicing in wind tunnels and on top of speeding vans. Today the tuck starts with skis far enough apart to ride flat, usually hip- or shoulder-width apart, depending on the shape of the skier's legs. The upper body is bent over so the chest rests on the knees. Upper arms rest in front of the shins, and hands are cupped against the face. The poles are curved to pass around the body, allowing the racer to get his hands together while the pole baskets ride in the wind-shadow behind the skier's butt. The position is easier to hold if you've a long trunk and short thighs; but even if you're built that way, it's still a tough pose to hold if you're banging over icy ruts at 70 mph. Holding your chest against the knees takes all the travel out of your suspension system.

Because of that, skiers must break out of the tuck to absorb big bumps and to land after being thrown through the air. A skier who can hold his tuck longer is likely to be a good deal faster, and a skier who keeps his skis on the snow stays closer to his chosen line—you simply can't steer with airborne skis. So every racer tries to minimize the amount of time he spends flying, using a technique called the prejump.

To understand the prejump, visualize what happens on a high-speed bump: the skier approaches from a relatively flat section (even if it's just a short compression), and his momentum is

On glide sections of a course, both giant slalom and downhill racers get into an aerodynamic "tuck" position. This drawing depicts a downhill racer in action.

therefore largely horizontal. The terrain suddenly falls away, faster than the skier can begin to fall. For a few, or several dozen, yards, the skier is airborne. But if the skier can absorb that bump with his knees, he won't be thrown so far through the air. Absorbing the bump means breaking out of the tuck early—"jumping" upward before the bump, while still on the flat. If he reaches full extension at just the right place, he can then absorb the bump by pulling the knees back up. This will place him back in his tuck at the crest of the bump and minimize the length of his flight. It requires fine timing, nerve, strength and experience.

The toughest parts of downhills are multiple bumps, which may not allow skiers to set up again after landing off the preceding bump. Another punishing problem is the fallaway high-speed turn, especially in icy conditions. The Hahnenkamm course at Kitzbühel, Austria, contains one such turn—Canadian downhiller Ken Read has compared it to "skiing around a bowling ball—you can't see where you're going and it feels like you can't get your edge in to get there." Watch carefully where a big bump is fol-

lowed by a sharp turn: the smoothest skiers will land early enough to set up properly for the turn. The fastest skiers, no matter how well they prejump, may sail into the curve and have to land on their edges, ready to turn hard.

The most critical skill is the ability to choose and hold a fast line. A racer can gain speed out of the starting gate by skating, but once he's reached 20 mph skating is out of the question. The only way he can gain speed out on the course is by letting his skis run with gravity, and that means pointing them down the fall line as often, and for as long, as possible. The fastest line is a carefully considered compromise between holding a clean, smooth turn and skiing straight downhill. It may be faster to come into a steep turn high, crank a short turn high on the bank and thus make the rest of the turn an accelerating straightaway. The fastest route through a flat turn will probably be a classic smooth long turn held in a low tuck. Racers are required, for safety, to

In the high-speed downhill race a prejump is executed prior to a fallaway transition to minimize airborne flight that would reduce a racer's speed.

practice for several days on any downhill course before the race; several dress-rehearsal races, called nonstops, are held in the days just before the event. The nonstops are used to find the right wax, the right skis—and the right line. But it's one thing to find the fast line in practice, and another to stick to it accurately during the race, when speeds may be considerably higher, or the snow conditions changed.

Courses, like skiers, may be regarded as gliding or technical in nature. Any course with a long, fairly flat section, or with few turns, is a gliding course, especially in soft snow. Any course that loops down very steep terrain is a technical course. A classic course should have both kinds of terrain, just as a master skier should glide and turn well. Most racers consider the Hahnenkamm, the Lauberhorn in Wengen, Switzerland, and the Streif in St. Anton, Austria, to be the great courses; the prestigious Arlberg-Kandahar races rotate between these sites. The annual World Cup schedule may include ten to fourteen downhills, including at least two in North America.

Downhill equipment is highly specialized. For high-speed stability, racers use long, wide skis—usually 223 or 225 cm for men, 213 or 215 cm for women. The skis are built with low, blunt tips for less air resistance, and sometimes the tips are lightened with holes. The lighter tip vibrates at a higher frequency, helping to break up surface tension in the film of water that forms under the ski base in soft snow. On hard, icy snow, skiers often select heavier, more stable skis. Suits fit skintight for low air-resistance, and the rules specify that helmets be worn. For maximum glide speed, the ski base must be selected and prepared to match the expected snow conditions—choosing the wrong ski or wax guarantees ignominy. Racers and coaches are therefore assisted by technicians, as skilled as race-car mechanics, who have studied the snow and weather conditions at downhill courses around the world and have prepared their skis accordingly. It's a high-pressure environment for everyone involved.

Because downhill skills are quite different from the skills required in slalom and giant slalom, downhill champions tend, with few exceptions, to be specialists—skiers who train for downhill and for no other event. To lure these specialists into the mainstream of Alpine ski racing, the World Cup added a new event during the early 1980s, the Super Giant Slalom, usually referred to simply as Super G. Super G was originally supposed to be a downhill with some very tight turns thrown in at the middle, but it was to be scored as a giant slalom. The idea was that downhillers could score giant slalom points in the race. As it evolved, however, Super G turned into a longer, faster giant slalom, and is often referred to as GS-in-one-run.

That's because it is scored as a giant slalom, and World Cup giant slalom proper is a two-run race. Racers ski one course in the morning, break for lunch, and those who completed the first run ski an adjacent course in the afternoon. Best combined time wins the event.

In English-speaking countries, giant slalom is most often referred to as GS. You'll frequently see the French or German equivalents on giant slalom skis: the French call it SG (for "slalom geant") and the Austrians call it RS (for "Riesenslalom"). GS courses are much shorter than downhills, dropping between 250 and 400 meters (820 to 1,300 feet) for men and between 250 and 350 meters for women (820 to 1,148 feet). The course is at least half-a-mile long, with gates set about 30 yards apart, usually in a predictable rhythmic pattern, but with a couple of trickier turns thrown in. GS will look familiar to recreational racers—the typical NASTAR course is set as a short, easy GS, with about the same gate spacing as used in World Cup giant slaloms.

GS demands clean, round turns, one after another. There are no straightaways. Speeds averages 30 to 35 mph and at this speed the skier must balance on a thin steel edge. Skid, and you'll finish at the back of the pack. GS is an event of intense concentration, because technique must be perfect. There are few gliders among great GS skiers—most have been

Three-time World Cup champ and Olympic gold medalist Phil Mahre dances through a maze of slalom gates at Kitzbühel's Hahnenkamm Combined in 1984. The rebound between turns has catapulted both skis clear of the snow, and he is about to land solidly on his right ski, already moving into the edged position for a hard left turn. *(Tom Lippert)*

expert technical skiers. Ingemar Stenmark, the Swede who has won more World Cup events than any racer in history, is widely regarded as the finest skier ever. He is a slalom-and-GS specialist—the ultimate technician.

You can tell at a glance whether you're watching a GS or a downhill because of the gate spacing and because GS skiers don't wear helmets. Otherwise, the skintight GS suit looks like the downhill suit. At these speeds—over 30 mph—aerodynamics are important, and when given the brief chance in a gentle turn, the racer will drop into a tuck. Aside from their spacing, GS gates differ from slalom gates visually: GS uses a double pole, with a rectangular flag stretched between the two wands, while slalom is a single pole with a small triangular flag. The GS ski is usually 210 cm long for men, 200 cm for women, and considerably narrower than the downhill ski, but because speed is important here, a GS ski is built with the same attention to vibration and base quality as the downhill. Glide speed is important to a GS racer, but downhill gliders don't often do well in GS simply because the course rarely allows them to flatten the ski and schuss. The ski has to glide fast on its edge, held in an accurate turn.

The confusion in GS arises from the two-run complication. As in all Alpine racing, skiers are "seeded"—faster racers, those standing higher in world ranking, are permitted to ski the course first, when the snow is relatively smooth and fast. In recent years priority in the second run has been given to those who finished well in the first run—that is, racers proceed in the order in which they finished the first run. The exception has been in the first five, who ski in reverse order.

This system has been deemed unfair to younger, relatively inexperienced racers of talent who may, given a clean course, be able to beat the current champs. So beginning with the 1984–1985 season, the World Cup used a "reverse 30" in certain races. Reverse 30 means that only the top 30 finishers in the first run move on to the second run, and they ski in reverse order. That gives finisher number 30 first shot at an unrutted course, and forces the winner of the first run to deal with whatever is left of the course. Some top skiers complained about it, but the best ones—like World Champion Erika Hess—proved able to win no matter where they started.

Slalom is the quickest, shortest race. A slalom course drops 140 to 200 meters (460 to 656 feet) for men, 120 to 180 meters (393 to 590 feet) for women—and the course must have fifty-five to seventy-five gates for men, forty to sixty gates for women. This means the skier encounters a gate about once each second at 15 mph. Slalom is not a sport for fine technique, it's a sport of explosive power and reaction time. Things happen so fast in a slalom course that it's tough to follow the action directly. The course looks like a maze of flags and you can best follow the skier's progress at a distance by watching the flags fall as the skier smashes past them.

But watch the skiers carefully and you'll see the same kind of variation in technique that's evident in downhill. Today slalom skiers tend to fall into two groups: classical skiers, who dance a smooth rhythm, leaping nimbly from edge-set to edge-set, skis flashing through the air between turns, and power skiers, who straighten out the line between gates, crash straight through the spring-loaded pole and jam a short, angular turn before aiming straight for the next gate. Power slalom is made possible by modern hinged gates, and participating skiers often wear padded sweaters, gauntlets on their gloves, fiberglass shin guards and helmets to protect themselves from impact with the pole. They dress, and ski, like pugilists, hands held high to fend off the blows.

The slalom ski is about 205 cm long for men, 190 cm for women, and is narrow in order to rock quickly from edge to edge. It's built not for ultimate glide speed but for ultimate tenacity on steep, icy snow.

Combined is a slippery event. In World Championship and Olympic racing, skiers run a special abbreviated downhill course and a special slalom course to earn medals in combined. But in the World Cup, combined points are calculated, on paper, based on finishes in paired events: a slalom and a downhill, or a slalom and a GS (the GS may actually be a Super G), or even a GS and a downhill. The combineds were created to encourage specialist downhillers and slalom experts to try the other events.

At the end of the season, all the points are added up and trophies are awarded for top points in slalom, giant slalom, downhill and overall. Until 1985, combined points counted toward a separate trophy, in spite of the fact that there was no combined race per se. As additional inducement to ski more than one type of event, only your top five finishes count in any discipline—so a skier can earn a maximum of 125 points in any one type of race. A perfect season would consist of five wins in slalom, five in GS and Super G, five in downhill and five in combined, for a total of 500 points. And still, the overall World Cup may very well go to a specialist. In eight of the past eleven

seasons, the overall World Cup for men has been won by slalom and GS specialists: Ingemar Stenmark, Phil Mahre and Marc Girardelli (Mahre, it's true, skied downhill when it would count for combined points, and Girardelli now does it, too). All the other winners— Jean-Claude Killy, Karl Schranz, Gustavo Thoeni, Piero Gros, Peter Luescher, Andreas Wenzel and Pirmin Zurbriggen— have been three-event skiers.

The women's World Cup is better balanced, since most women ski all three events. But even there most winners tend to have a single strength: Nancy Greene dominated GS, Marie-Therese Nadig and Maria Walliser were powerful in downhill, Annemarie Proell Moser and Michela Figini were hot in downhill and GS while Lise-Marie Morerod and Tamara McKinney were tops in slalom and GS. Erika Hess, Hanni Wenzel, Rosi Mittermaier and Gertrud Gabl are or were well-rounded skiers but were most consistent in slalom.

The season ends each spring with a final parallel slalom. It counts not for World Cup individual points but for team, or Nations Cup, points. A parallel slalom is simply a side-by-side race course with two skiers racing each other down theoretically identical courses. After one run, they swap courses to even out any inequity in terrain. It's fun to watch and very exciting for racers and spectators.

Regardless of the type of race, every World Cup skier bursts out of the starting gate with a characteristic explosion. Invented by Jean-Claude Killy, the World Cup start is meant to get the racer's upper body moving well away even before his feet trip the starting wand, triggering the clock. It works like this: the racer plants his poles in the snow just downhill from the starting wand, and

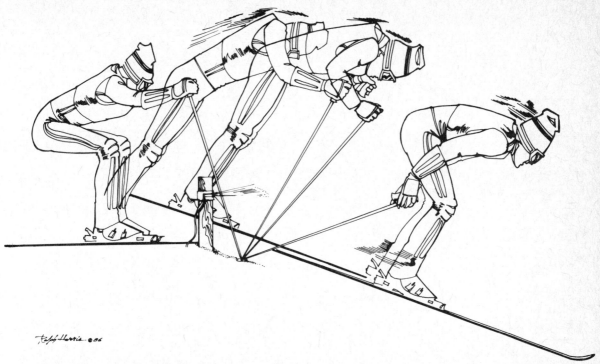

The flying start, universal among World Cup Alpine racers. The start gives the skier significant forward momentum before the race starter signals "go."

then crouches back on his skis, knees and waist bent—he looks as if he's sitting in a chair. As the starter's count nears "Go!" the racer's upper body begins moving forward, like a spring uncoiling. A second before the signal to go, he kicks downward, extending his upper body and launching it up and over the wand. One leg goes up and back as the skier's weight comes on his arms and poles; then the other. The skier pushes down and back on his poles, propelling the upper body forward to achieve almost a full lay-out position. From the knees up, the racer has extended out beyond the starting wand, and he's already generated considerable momentum toward the first gate; and his feet have not yet reached the starting wand. Plunging out and

downward, the racer must finally bring his feet forward through the wand just at the word "Go!" to catch his fall—which has now been converted into forward motion. It looks smooth and wonderful in practice, but neophyte racers—and occasionally the experts—will trip the start wand before the signal to go and be disqualified. Essentially, the flying start is a standing broad jump done on skis and aimed downhill. It gains the racer nearly a second over the old-fashioned standing start, in which the racer simply shuffles through the wand and then begins skating toward the first gate. Because of that time advantage, the flying start is in universal use among World Cup racers.

The basis of both slalom and GS techniques is the racing step turn (see page 127, Chapter 9), so-called because it involves stepping uphill onto the new ski and then rolling it over to establish the new turn. In effect, this is a skating motion, and can, especially in slalom, produce a net gain in speed on each gate. In GS it's used primarily to establish a smoother, wider radius path to the next gate—the step is uphill, but it's also lateral, and may gain the skier a three-foot advantage in lining up with the fall line en route to the next pole.

Skating has recently come to dominate cross-country World Cup racing, too. It turns out that it's faster to skate around a firm-packed track than to kick-and-glide, and so the traditionalists at all distances—15 km, 30 km and 50 km for men, 5 km, 10 km and 20 km for women—were decimated. The established Nordic nations—the Scandinavians and Russians—howled, with the confusing result that since the 1985–1986 season half the World Cup cross-country races were "freestyle" or skating events and half were "classic" kick-and-glide races. At the World Cup level, cross-country is a remarkable event. Top men typically skate a 15 km race in 38 minutes. That's about 13 mph, roughly equivalent to running 9 miles at 4 minutes and 5 seconds per mile.

Naturally, the cross-country World Cup has been dominated by Scandinavians and Russians—men's winners have been Ivar Formo, Oddvar Braa, Juha Mieto, Thomas Wassberg, Sven-Ake Lundback, Alexander Zavjalov, Gunde Svan and—happily—American Bill Koch. Koch is significant because he, more than anyone else, proved skating a faster style. Women's winners have been Galina Kulakova, Raisa Smetanina, Berit Aunli, Marja-Liisa Hamalainen, Anette Boe, and Marjo Matikainen.

The World Cup cross-country schedule is no less exacting than the Alpine tour: men and women both ski a total of sixteen races. Men's races are run at 15 km, 30 km and 50 km, plus a 40 km relay run in four 10 km stages. Women's events are run at 5 km, 10 km and 30 km, with a 20 km relay in four 5 km stages.

"It's a grueling schedule, and the need to train for both skating and diagonal skiing makes it tougher," notes Koch. "On the World Cup circuit, you usually spend Monday traveling, or Monday and Tuesday if the race is in an Eastern bloc country. Tuesday through Thursday, you work out on the track. That usually means one day of long distance skiing at a fast pace—if it's a 15 kilometer race, I'd go 50 kilometers at near-race speed. The other two days would be interval training. On Friday you test skis to see what's running well and what wax to use. Then it always snows Friday night and changes everything. Saturday and Sunday you ski two races, a solo event and a relay. The trick is to keep the hard training coming. Once you get cranking, the racing itself really takes care of the training program."

Not many people can keep up this kind of pace all winter long, but Koch believes a few more races could be added to the schedule, to accommodate skaters, "without making the racers get sick."

"If more skating events are added, the top skiers will begin to specialize in skating, and it will gradually kill diagonal," he said. "Skating is still evolving, but it's already so much faster than diagonal skiing that if you took the top 50 citizen finishers of the Bierkie and transplanted them back one year, they could have done well at the World Championships. As skating technique continues to improve, you'll see the top skiers go *minutes*

Audun Endestad (left) of the U.S. Ski Team, and Oddvar Braa, the great Norwegian Olympian, sprint for the finish of the 1986 American Bierkebeiner Marathon. *(Bierkebeiner Staff Photo)*

faster every year for the next five winters. And the guys who push skating hardest will reap the rewards."

World Cup trophies are now also awarded for jumping and Nordic Combined, which rewards combined scores in cross-country and jumping. Jumping is spectacular fun to watch. A modern jump hill is an imposing feature of the landscape. It consists of a steep inrun

ramp, usually built on an artificial tower, ending in a flat take-off that sends the jumper flying over a steep outrun slope, usually a hillside bulldozed to the right shape.

A typical inrun slopes at about 40 degrees, and if it's a 90-meter jump, it is long enough to launch skiers at 55 to 60 mph, equivalent to downhill speeds; on a 90-meter hill, good form at this speed should produce a jump of well over 300 feet (World Cup competition is also held on 70-meter hills, where top jumpers go about 250 feet, and on huge ski flying hills, where distances over 600 feet are common). The outrun of the jump is profiled so that the jumper is never more than 10 or 12 feet from the ground, and the landing is therefore made at a shallow angle. Beginning about 10 feet under the take-off, the outrun is flat. It quickly steepens to an angle equal to the pitch of the inrun ramp, then arcs gradually to a flat finish area with a counter-hill to slow speeding skiers to a stop. Falls on landing are not uncommon, and may be horrific, but skiers are seldom hurt. What's dangerous is flying beyond the steep landing zone into the flat finish area, where the heavy impact at a high angle can hurt a jumper seriously.

Aerodynamics are crucial to jumping. The current style—body arcing far forward over the ski tips, arms held back in a delta with hands spread as ailerons—has been evolved to maximize lift, to extend the jump distance. Working in wind tunnels, modern jumpers have learned to angle their jumps slightly, returning to the straight-ahead position just in time to land in the classic telemark posture. This sideslip through the air—it looks like a small plane crabbing in to a cross-wind landing—turns the skis themselves into high-aspect-ratio airfoils, like long slim wings, instead of the short, stubby, low-aspect wings they would be straight ahead.

Jump scoring needs as much explanation as Alpine World Cup scoring. Jumpers get style points as well as distance points. Style points are meant to assure everyone that the skier at least knows how to land safely—if he's unsteady in the air and on landing, he

doesn't have much chance to win even if he launched at such an out-of-control speed that he tumbles farther than everyone else. Each jumper gets a practice jump and two scored jumps. On each scored jump, each of five judges can award a jumper up to 20 points for style—five judges with 20 points each means 100 possible points. But to eliminate bias, the high and low scores are thrown out, leaving just three middle scores. So a perfect style score is 60 points. Distance points are calculated according to where the jumper lands relative to the "table point," a line drawn across the hill in the middle of the safe landing area. The table point is worth 60 points—jumps beyond it score higher, and short jumps score lower. The end of the safe landing zone—the point where the outrun begins to flatten out, and where a landing would therefore produce a heavy impact, is called the critical point. When a skier lands beyond the critical point, the judges conclude that takeoff speeds are too high for safety, and the starting point for the inrun is moved downward. The beginning of the safe landing area is called the norm point. On a 90-meter hill, the norm point is 90 meters from the take-off. After the style and distance points are added up for two scored jumps, a good score should total around 250 points.

A jump works like this: the skier crouches on a flat platform alongside the inrun ramp, holding on to a railing. When officials judge the wind conditions to be safe, he's signaled to go (many jumpers will wait for a favorable headwind for additional lift—it's the sidewinds that are dangerous). Using the railing as a push-off, the jumper leaps out onto the inrun and hops his skis around to point straight down the narrow track, dropping into an aerodynamic tuck. At the bottom of the inrun, the track levels out into a flat take-off. Here the jumper leaps up and forward, arching out over his skis. The perfect take-off is timed to achieve full extension just as the feet pass over the lip, but it's safer to leap late than early; an early extension can drop the ski tips, and if the wind catches the tips and pulls them down . . . that's a sorry skier, turning slowly, slowly in the wind.

With a good position, and at a normal 60 mph speed, the skier is really flying, controlling his position aerodynamically, like a stable skydiver. Today, jumpers spend hours in wind tunnels to learn flying control. In years past, before wind tunnels were made available to jumpers, a skier could jump for years and his accumulated flying time might only add up to a couple of hours, gained 3 to 6 seconds at a time. Now a skier can learn what he needs to know in an hour of hanging in a wind tunnel, and then spend several hours each summer back in the wind tunnel rehearsing his position until the take-off and control movements are second-nature. The result is vastly improved distance and safety.

Ski jumping equipment is unique. Jumping skis are even much wider and longer than downhill skis—typically 240 cm long and about 12.7 cm wide. The low, aerodynamic tips are carefully beveled to reduce turbulence, and the slick plastic bases contain four or five deep grooves to help the ski glide straight and true on the inrun. The sides of the skis are parallel—there is no sidecut, because the skis are designed only to go straight and glide flat. For the same reason, jumping skis do not have steel edges. Jumping boots look something like telemark boots—like telemark boots they bend at the ball of the foot and are stiff laterally and torsionally, so the skier can control the direction of the ski even with the heel lifted. But jumping boots are built up high and stiff behind the lower leg, to help the skier maintain his balance on landing.

As in Alpine skiing, Nordic World cups award 25 points for a win. The comparability of scores provokes this speculation: if a way could be found, through the complex schedules, for a few modern Skimeisters to compete in both Alpine and Nordic World Cup races, a Total Skier World Cup trophy might be awarded for combined scores in a slalom, downhill, cross-country race and jump. During 1987, for instance, it would have been possible for a skier to compete in the 90-meter jump at Garmisch, West Germany, on January 1, the 15 km freestyle cross-country at Calgary, Alberta, on January 8, and the slalom-downhill combined at Wengen, Switzerland, January 17-18, all without missing another Alpine race, if he were an Alpine skier, or cross-country race, if he were a runner.

That January triathlon doesn't exist—yet—but if it's ever held, the winner would be the skier's skier of the year.

Downhill skiing brings out the free spirit; skiers dance and pirouette down the slope or fly through the air. *(Bob Jonas)*

11
Freestyle

Call it craziness or call it art, freestyle skiing is certainly unconventional. The freestyle skier is not content just to ski down the mountain; he wants to dance, to swoop, to fly.

Most accomplished Alpine skiers derive satisfaction in linking shortswing turns in fluid style down an intermediate slope. The freestyle skier pirouettes, dances or glides on a single ski. The skilled skier relishes conquering a big mogul field nonstop without a fall. The freestyle skier attacks that mogul field with speed and boldness, jumping, twisting and slicing through bumps as fast as possible. The competent skier, slipping over the lip of a cornice or a big bump executes a fine *gelände* (terrain jump). The freestyle skier sweeps by, jetting out into space, spreading the skis wide before flipping head over heels to a landing. Freestyle is rock 'em, sock 'em skiing at its best.

The sport of Alpine skiing encourages free spirits and freedom of movement. There have always been and always will be skiers who waltz and pirouette down the slopes, crash through moguls and sail through the air. In the 1960s a few adventuresome American skiers transformed stunt skiing into a new kind of competition. They became performers, calling themselves *hot dogs*.

More formally, they called their sport freestyle skiing.

Perhaps more than any other skier, Norway's Stein Ericksen inspired the new generation of American freestylers. Ericksen, a double gold medalist in the 1952 Winter Olympics, was a gymnast, a skill that enabled him to thread the tight slalom course with the quickness and balance of a cat, to ski the open slopes with uncommon grace. But Stein became better known in this country for his famous somersaults on skis, somersaults executed with a perfection that made his name synonymous with graceful, beautiful skiing. To ski downhill like Stein was and still is a standard for recreational skiers.

But the real springboard contributing to the meteoric rise of the modern freestylers was the appearance of a special shorter ski designed by American ski instructor Clif Taylor. Taylor wanted to give his students a very maneuverable ski, to help make skiing easier and faster to learn. Suddenly, the free spirits had a ski on which they could pivot on a dime, or on the crown of a mogul, turning again before hitting the next mogul.

By the early seventies America's hotdogs had become full-time entertainers on skis. They exploded down through the bumps rather than skiing around

A Royal Christy turn, a freestyle maneuver executed by lifting one ski off the snow. *(Bob Jonas)*

them. They didn't just fly off jumps, but spun, turned and walked through the air. On smooth intermediate slopes they did intricate figure skating movements on one or two skis. As they competed to see who could top whom, organized freestyle skiing was born. Competition soon separated into three events: ballet, mogul and aerials.

THE EVENTS

Ballet Skiing

Ballet skiing is performed on easy, groomed, intermediate slopes. The ski used in ballet is short and flexible, enabling the skier to perform precise tricks. Ballet skiing began as figure skating on skis. The moves are like those performed on ice: gliding on one leg, dancing, axles, and inside and outside spins on one or both feet. The basic moves later evolved into heel and toe spins and flips performed over the top of the ski poles.

Today the poles are longer, and the skis even shorter. This combination allows more inverted maneuvers, including forward and backward twisting flips and cartwheels. While moving downslope, skiers can do triple spins. Though the classic skating moves still exist, there are more tricks involved than before. A well-executed difficult maneuver will receive high points from the judges.

Each competitor's routine is performed over the same distance on a slope several hundred yards long. The choreography and music are chosen by each individual skier. As in skating, judges hold up placards with numerals awarding points based on style, tricks and overall performance. The prime prerequisites for ballet skiing are balance, flexibility and gymnastic ability.

Aerial Skiing

Aerial skiing is worlds apart from ballet skiing. Aerials require a special arena, a jump constructed exclusively for aerials, as well as a steep, smooth slope for landing. The jumps have evolved into mammoth structures in order for the jumper to get enough time in the air to perform

Ballet is like figure skating on skis—performed to music, it's a graceful, gymnastic dance. *(Hart Ski Company)*

variations on multiple somersaults or to execute a quadruple flip. At a contest, there are several jumps of varying sizes from which the skier will leap according to the demands of his aerial stunt. The aerialist's skis are short to accommodate the tumbling twists and somersaults incorporated in the jump.

Originally aerialists flew upright, performing spread eagles with the legs spread wide; back scratchers, with ski tips dropped, the tails touching an arched back; daffies, or sky walking; and double and triple helicopters, or spins.

Later, dangerous inverted jumps began to dominate the aerials: front layouts and back layouts; front flips and back flips; single twisting flips and doubles, front and back; triple flips—with twists, of course. Then came the milestone quadruple flip. The aerialist today is a master gymnast. To gain the final round in a competition, the competitor can't afford to attempt a less than spectacular upright jump. The uprights are simply not difficult or impressive enough to win judging points. In the final round, the competition begins with triples, front or back. Each skier has only three jumps, and the maneuvers must be spectacular if the jumper is to win.

Moguls

A moguled slope appears to be a sea of hives, one bump followed by another. A mogul field is intimidating seen from its edge, straight down. It's steep and requires a lot of quick turns. The bumps are spaced a stride apart and are often waist high. The downhill side of each bump is a chopped off face separated from the next bump by a banana-shaped trough. Landing in the trough can be a body-crunching experience. Negotiating the field means finding a route through chaos.

The mogul freestyler must be a superior downhill skier, technically perfect (see photo sequence, pages 160–161). He must have extraordinary balance and be very quick. Finally, the skier must be able to execute turns smoothly, or the difficulty of moguled terrain will wear the skier down.

The winner of an early mogul competition used to be the most flamboyant and original skier. Alone, the competitor bashed down through the moguls executing a variety of spins and even flips. If the skier survived a spectacular run without falling, usually he received the nod of both judges and the crowd. Today, the mogul competition is much more controlled. The winner is simply the best mogul skier, not necessarily the best exhibitionist on skis.

The competitive format is more exacting—and exciting. No longer is it possible for a less than excellent skier to place high. The skier must not only demonstrate turning and bump jumping artistry, but must beat the other skier to the bottom of the slope.

The skiers race two at a time on parallel courses—the slope is neatly bisected into two corridors by loosely spaced, flagged poles. A superior competitor gets one point for aerial artistry off the bumps, two for the best turns and one for finishing first. A fifth point is awarded for overall mastery. But the race to beat the other skier to the finish is what creates the intense pressure that the spectators feel.

"The head to head competition is a real adrenaline rush," says Joey Cordeau. "You can feel the other guy right there."

"We wanted to be sure the best skier won the mogul event," says Joey, three time professional mogul king and instrumental in the reorganization of the mogul competition. "It's not show anymore, it's competition."

The dual format has caused the competitors to rein in the theatrics; the first order of business is to beat your opponent to the bottom. Jumping still provides excitement, but the skiers are conservative, risking airborne antics only a few times late in a good run, once a fast finish is assured. There is a premium now on what Cordeau labels "ultimate skiing," the ability to go very fast on the most demanding terrain.

Joey is a Stein of the moguls, a skier of liquid grace. Despite his speed in the bumps, his moves are quiet and silken, a breeze flowing gently over humped, spiny terrain. He is a soft stroke instead of a jarring slash.

Cordeau stands tall with his feet together when he skis, moving in a controlled quick rhythm. "In the bumps I arch my turns like I do on a flat run—no noise, smoothly. I like the feeling of good technique."

Joey skis 120 days each winter, making four out of every five runs in the bumps, on what may be the best bump mountain in the world, Sun Valley's Baldy. "I'm at home in the bumps," says Cordeau. "I'll be doing it for another ten years."

Of the three freestyle disciplines the moguls are a skier's event. Moguls challenge the skier with what skiing is about: a long descent over the intricacies of terrain. Aerials and ballet have evolved from skier's play into highly specialized gymnastic contests isolated in spirit from mountain skiing. Ex-gymnasts win in ballet and aerials; ex–ski racers win in the bumps.

Inverted aerial stunts are thrilling to watch and dangerous to perform. *(Bob Jonas)*

It is high tribute to one's athletic ability if you are able to enter all three events and do well (a combined award that crowns the overall winner in freestyle skiing competitions does encourage participation in all three events).

FREESTYLE HISTORY

Something as flashy and spirited as competitive freestyle skiing, which exploded into being as a new way of having fun, is bound to have a checkered history. Freestyle competition was launched in Amer-

ica in the first years of the seventies, but had slipped toward oblivion here by mid-decade. Still popular in Europe, it is only now making a tenuous comeback in the U.S., although a renaissance in the sport is expected: freestyle skiing will be a demonstration event for the 1988 Winter Olympics.

What happened to freestyle skiing in America? In the beginning the gregarious fun-loving freestylers commanded attention. They were the new skiing sensation and everyone loved to watch them. Media attention, ski industry sponsorship and corporate money soon followed.

Freestyle meant freedom. It was Woodstock on the mountain; perhaps a last chapter of the rootless sixties. The competitors were wired to their Astraltunes, the prototype Walkman personal stereo. Music blared from on-mountain speakers. The abandon was infectious for both crowd and competitors.

Tall, red-haired Penelope Street, a champion freestyle skier of the early years, recalls them this way: "It started for me at Lake Louise, Canada. I was teaching skiing. I was down to my last cord of wood, jar of honey and box of oatmeal. This guy shows up and says how would you like to be a hot dogger, all expenses paid. I said sure.

"A lot of good skiers, bored with Alpine downhill, got into hot dogging," Penelope recalls. "They were all good in the moguls. They became ballet skiers and jumpers. In my first event, a ballet, I placed one hundred third out of one hundred five. But it was fun to learn, and I was able to get to the top fast."

Penelope liked all the events, but she liked the moguls best. "Moguls cover more distance and there is more time for spontaneous creativity. We loved going down those terrible, hacking, giant

In the modern freestyle mogul competition, competitors meet head to head. Beating the competition to the bottom of the slope is one factor determining the overall winner. *(Gary Brettnacher)*

moguls. It was like a controlled free-fall. We touched our feet down now and then to kind of control our speed so we would not rocket straight to the bottom. The crowd howled and the music was electric. You were completely out of breath at the bottom. It was a high."

When the money started coming into the sport, so too came the specialists, highly trained gymnasts from outside the ski world. "They were hacker skiers who could spin and twirl, gymnasts who were aerial artists only," says Penelope.

But it was the antics of the free-stylers themselves, more than anything, that brought an end to the early years of the sport. Eventually, the lure of money brought in very young and headstrong competitors willing to go too far. Out to win money and responding to the whoop and razz of the crowd, skiers got wild. They injured themselves on the moguls while skiing too fast and performing at the edge of control. The aerials became a show of oneupmanship—flips were taken to their limits. Jumps were built with ramps that literally stopped the feet and flung the accelerating skier forward into the air in a somersault. Single flips gave way to doubles and triples. Controls were not always tight. Inevitably, there were injuries. Several top competitors were paralyzed. To pay their medical bills, most of them sued their ski industry sponsors.

Insurance companies responded by raising premiums and writing exclusions against inverted aerials. Ski area management, already concerned with the "long hair" reputation of freestyle skiing, found the threat of liability suits outrageous. Soon few ski areas were willing to host contests, and the freestyle circuit died. As the money dried up, competing freestyle circuits filed suits against one anothers' sponsors, causing the corporations (and television) to withdraw from the sport. The hot doggers looked for real jobs.

But the aura of freedom surrounding freestyle never died and the sport was flourishing abroad. In Europe, the carefree flamboyant Americans of the early freestyle era struck a chord that has swept the continent. While freestyle was languishing in America, the Europeans embraced it wholeheartedly. Today, European national freestyle teams have the support of their governments. It is the Europeans who created the push toward incorporating freestyle into the Winter Olympics. Freestyle skiing also enjoys a solid reputation in Canada, and Canada, too, has a national team.

In America today, there are once again freestyle skiing events. Amateur freestyle competition in America is under the tight control and sanction of the USSA. There is also a separate professional competition in the moguls, though prize money is limited.

Like many sports, freestyle competition has evolved into disciplined, refined athletic performance. The standards continue to be raised in each of the events.

LEARNING TO FREESTYLE

Before attempting any serious aerial skiing, it is an absolute prerequisite that you obtain expert instruction and are specifically trained in order to avoid injury. If you were to land incorrectly following a flip, you could seriously injure yourself. The height an aerialist has to jump to do a triple flip, for example, is scary just to behold. Snow can be very hard. You want to land upright after your aerial stunt. The human body is not meant to plummet fifty feet in the air and land headfirst. Aerial skiing is more dangerous than, say, trampoline, because there are no spotters to catch an out-of-control athlete.

Ballet skiing is safer, but again, it is best to seek professional instruction and advice. The USSA, which sanctions amateur freestyle meets today and establishes the safety standards governing the sport, is the best place to start to find out where freestyle training is available. Another option is some of the summer training camps in America and Europe; several provide basic instruction. *Ski* magazine lists these camps yearly in the camp directory included in its April (spring) issue.

MOGUL SKIING TECHNIQUE

While very few skiers ever become competitive aerialists or ballet skiers, the challenge of skiing the moguls exists on every lift-served mountain. Moguls quickly form on a slope with the passage of successive skiers. Left alone, every slope would become a forest of bumps growing taller, tighter and more difficult by the day. Machined slope grooming clears the daily accumulation. But some steep slopes are never leveled by the

1   2   3   4

snowcat fleets. It is these slopes, where the moguls become monsters, that present a special challenge to the lift-served skier.

The bumps on steep slopes today are much different from those in the past. The moguls formed used to be long, round and rhythmic, carved by skiers on long skis. The line through the bumps was a clear one. Today, the quick-turning high performance shorter skis used by the better technical skiers slash across the steep slopes and carve moguls into an unrelenting wave of mini-cliffs. Most skiers ski around each bump, accentuating the troughs between the moguls, and making the cliff faces even taller.

Today's bumps on the steep slopes are a challenge unlike anything else on the mountain. If you can ski the big bumps, you'll be a master terrain skier, able to handle any mountain with ease; and you'll be a better citizen racer. Even if you don't tackle the big hummocks on the steep, you will still need to acquire some bump skills for the lower slopes.

One of the reasons the big bump slopes are difficult to ski is that the line through them is not so obvious as it is

In these photo sequences, three-time World Pro Mogul Champion Joey Cordeau demonstrates his big bump ski technique. Note that Cordeau skis *on* each mogul instead of skiing *around* the mogul and into the trough separating moguls.

In photo 1, Cordeau slides *across* the trough between moguls; in photo 2 he prepares to use the avalement absorption technique *on top* of the mogul; in photo 3 he absorbs the mogul coming over its crest; in photos 4–7 he turns on the *face* of the mogul; and in photo 8, he skis across the trough.

In photo 9, Cordeau absorbs the mogul on its crown; in photo 10 he turns on the face; in photo 11 he rebounds down and across the trough; and in photo 12 he prepares to absorb the next bump.

(All photos John Plummer)

while racing through gates or while open-slope skiing in lesser moguls. And while you can turn out of a gate course and stop after blowing a turn, you can get into big trouble if you don't stick with a bump line. In the moguls, there is no opportunity to recover; you must turn very quickly and very often, constantly seeking the "smooth spot" on the next bump. You must be very well centered.

Co-author Bob Jonas writes: "When I returned to bump skiing after several

5   6   7   8

9   10   11   12

years' absence, I tried skiing the line *around* the bump as I had always done. In the past the bumps were shaped like a ship's prow and were easy to ski around. In the new bumps, when I weighted the skis forward, the tails of my long skis caught in the bananalike troughs, hooking my tips into chopped faces. The skis literally sailed out from under me when I used avalement absorption technique in the deep troughs."

In the avalement posture the skier is sitting back, the weight shifting toward the heels. In the old moguls you could down-unweight in this posture, absorbing the occasional hole below the mogul, while changing edges for the next turn. Because the edging in avalement occurs under the foot and toward the tail of the ski—as opposed to forward of the feet—you gained reaction time, "stalling" the turn while you "fishtailed" between tight bumps with a hole, like a waterskier slaloming on his tails. Avalement is still very important in modern big-bump technique, but it is not used in the trough. In an arched, deep trough, avalement causes the ski tips, hence the skis, to go up and away.

"Ninety percent of skiers today ski the troughs and that's wrong," Joey Cordeau says. "It ruins the moguls by forming the tight bump and the big face. They should stay *out* of the hole."

Joey's suggestion may shake up the teaching establishment. Skiing the trough is taught as effective skiing by most instructors. Sometimes the line *is* around the moguls. This is usually true with small moguls on lesser slopes, or when the moguls are first created after grooming. But when the bumps are big and the trough is deep, you may need to break with convention. Cordeau's advice:

"I look for the smooth spot, taking each mogul as a separate mountain. When it goes up you had better be going up; when it goes down, you should be going down. The key is to stay on the snow—not in the air. If you don't you're smacking and absorbing the shock. The skis will absorb ninety percent of the shock if you're doing it right."

While most bump skiers use a slalom ski with a soft tip, deep sidecut and still tail, Cordeau prefers a 205 giant slalom ski. He likes the wide waist and more forgiving tail of the giant slalom ski. A GS ski is damp for shock absorption as opposed to being quick or extremely responsive. "Soon as you initiate a slalom ski it goes; a GS you have to push through the bumps," Cordeau says. "It stays put. The slalom ski is more fidgety."

Cordeau's line is directly down the fall line. It seems as if he smacks from crown to crown on the bumps, but that overlooks his subtlety. In fact, he flows over the moguls, catching the smooth spot on the backside here, the flank there, part of a face. He skis *on* the bump instead of around it in the trough. "Go over the bad spot if you have to; then when you're in the clear, make some quick turns, two or three depending upon the size of the upcoming mogul. If you get caught in the trough, you can't put much weight, if any, on the tips or tails—you'd be thrown out if you do. You absolutely have to be looking ahead, not at what you're going over."

Skiing the big bumps is like racing a slalom course in the bumps. The gate combinations are tricky and very tight. You won't be able to study the line beforehand; you have to find it as you go.

No racer would run a course without previously studying it, nor should you. Learn the techniques on the smaller moguls. Cordeau suggests that skiers "learn how to arc and rebound with the skis, and know how to push." Arcing refers to a firm touch that turns the ski, but not so firmly that the ski hooks into the bump. You have to get off the edge quickly. Fear in the big bumps makes skiers want to hold the edge, and that can be disastrous.

The rebound and push Cordeau refers to is really terrain absorption—avalement technique (see photo sequences on pages 160–161). Your legs in the moguls are loaded springs. If you hit the upside or flank of a big mogul at high speed while standing up, you can end up crashing or caroming into another bump. The solution is to let the ski take the hit, loading the legs down briefly in anticipation (avalement absorption), then unloading instantly in a rebound while the skis are still quivering with the hit.

"I go through five pairs of skis in a season, but I've never been hurt skiing the bumps, not an ache or a pain," Cordeau says. Luckily, he has a major ski company to sponsor his bump skiing and keep him supplied with fresh skis. But his point is a good one.

On the downside of the mogul, pick up the transition between bumps by coming down softly, like a cat, pushing lightly, then spring quickly away on the rebound. You do not have to change your body position. By all means *stay out of the hole.*

Remember—you cannot be tentative in the bumps. Get an expert to show you the smooth spots in a mogul field, where to ski and where not to ski.

Extreme skier Kim Anderson demonstrates the technique for skiing slopes beyond 40 degrees pitch. *(Jock Leavin)*

12
Variations

On the thin edge, at the limit of the possible in the world of skiing, the universe slows down. It's a matter of perception, of course: when adrenaline supercharges the brain, thoughts crowd in between events and seem to push them apart, stretching out time. Adrenaline junkies thrive on this time dilation. Your skis become a time machine when you take them into mortal danger.

Kim Anderson is one of a select few addicted to steep skiing.

"Extreme skiing starts at forty-five degrees; you must climb up," Kim explains. He has a single criterion to govern whether a slope is skiable: he must be able to stand on it, unroped.

Kim's is a world of 60-degree pitches, thousands of feet long. Sylvain Saudan and Patrick Vallencant, cult figures in Europe, have made careers of ski extreme—Kim is one of the few Americans who skis at this angle. To put it in perspective, a sustained 15-degree slope is considered an advanced trail at any American ski area; 20 degrees is expert terrain; 30 degrees is prime avalanche hazard; 40 degrees is unskiable by conventional techniques. Extend your arm and put your palm flat against the wall. A string stretched from your foot to your hand rises at 60 degrees. Take that angle and ski it in a couloir—a "snow run" or avalanche chute, a very narrow gully slashed vertically in the rock face of a high mountain. You find couloirs where sheer rock faces are crumbling into the eons. They are elevator shafts down which chunks of eroded rock hurtle, where falling snow cannot hold on. A sane person won't stand in a couloir, let alone ski it. In the couloir, each turn is an exercise in mental bankruptcy, and failure can mean death. You will ricochet off the stony flanks of the couloir, gaining speed until disgorged far below, beyond the foot of the rock.

Kim Anderson skis in the couloir, poised for the turn, his skis bowed, tips and tails hanging in the funnel of snow. Before taking off, he perches like a bird of prey, head bobbing, crouched, focus intent downslope. Then, explosively, he launches, windmilling 180 degrees to land in the opposite direction, testing the precarious footing of a new perch. Turn by turn he drops, until the couloir opens out and the man can finally link his turns with caution.

Anderson is the consummate Total Skier. He enjoys all skiing, but credits ski extreme for focusing his life. "I was looking for something else, something new, another thrill beyond Alpine or freestyle skiing," he says. "The actual skiing is an electrical rush, the biggest I've ever had.

When you're falling out of the air ten or fifteen feet on every turn, that is a rush. You are airborne, unattached to the earth for seconds on every turn. It's definitely better than flips on skis. It's another way to reach higher levels of consciousness."

In 1985 Kim sought to be the first American to ski the east face of the Eiger, whose North Wall is the most feared and sought-after trophy in all of technical climbing. After weeks of waiting, and of being avalanched off the mountain, he called it quits. "Something was telling me I shouldn't be there," he says.

He has skied off the summit of the Grand Teton in Wyoming—twice. Twice, because he fell in the notorious Stettner Couloir the first time. Part of the couloir is skiable, but one bottleneck has to be down-climbed, and a traverse made onto a skiable slope to avoid the cliff before the descent can resume. Kim tried to ski the bottleneck. That he is alive is simple luck. But he had to prove to himself that his confidence was not eroded. Hence a second, successful attempt.

"The Grand Teton fall was a turning point in my life," Kim says. "It was the second time I saw my life pass before me, the first being when I tried to do a triple flip on skis. I had to ski the Grand again, not just for the sake of the descent, but for courage in life. Extreme skiing has become a spiritual thing." He now considers the Grand a good training mountain, and the litmus test for any would-be extreme skier. The next time he does the Grand, he says, it will be solo—unassisted on the climb, completely alone.

The descent he is proud of is Artesonrajau, in Peru. The mountain stands like a shark's tooth, clean, tearing the sky. There are no couloirs on the side Kim skied, just a naked, relentlessly steep face. At the 20,000-foot summit, he re-leased his umbilical, stepping away from rope and crampons. He had to chop out a perch on the face where he could sit while taking ski boots and skis out of his pack, putting them on, snapping into the bindings. Then he could stand there in the sky, looking downward at over a mile of exposure, as his climbing partners began to rope down.

The only other skier to have skied this descent is Vallencant, who made a very entertaining film about Artesonrajau. Vallencant and Saudan make a very good living out of ski extreme. Kim wouldn't mind that kind of success, but only because the money could support his habit. He talks constantly about extraordinary dimensions—about time dilation. "In those split seconds when I detach from the earth I enter another dimension, then come back to reality," he says. "The object is to remain in that other dimension. Someday I would like to fly to the top."

To find out how it's even possible to ski on snow steeper than 50 degrees, co-author Seth Masia traveled to Les Arcs, in the Tarentaise range of the French Alps, and spent a week with Alain Gaimard, a friend and rival of Vallencant. Gaimard runs a school of extreme skiing centered on Arc 2000, an incredible natural amphitheater three miles long and a mile wide, boxed in by 10,000-foot peaks with 3,000-foot couloirs. The couloir is Gaimard's classroom. "Good skiers come here with an inflated sense of what they can and have skied," Gaimard says. "One guy came to me saying he could ski forty-five degrees. We put him on forty and he fell off. So the first thing a student learns is humility with the mountain. The penalty for a mistake is very severe in ski extreme, so you must not try what you may not be able to do."

The "pedal-jump turn" is the three-step technique for extreme skiing. First, the skier plants the pole far down slope; second, the skier leaps into space with the *downhill* ski; third, he follows with the uphill ski while pivoting around the pole plant to a stop.

Very steep slopes don't hold snow well. When snow is fresh, every time you turn you kick off a small slough, so there's always a lot of loose snow tumbling around your feet. To avoid starting a real avalanche the turn has to be very smooth and controlled. The technique developed for ski extreme is the pedal-jump turn.

It starts one ski at a time—with the downhill ski. Think of it as a racing step in reverse. Gaimard describes it as a three-step dance: one, plant the pole far down the hill; two, step off into space with the downhill ski; three, follow with the uphill ski, pivoting around the pole to land gently, feet together, at a dead stop and facing in the other direction. Test the snow for sliding, and if it's safe, pedal jump again.

The skis don't slide forward much in this turn, which means, if your skis are 204 cm long, you can ski a couloir about 210 cm wide. But Gaimard started the class off on a very wide, very short and extremely steep 55-degree pitch under a small cornice. There was vertical room to make just two or three turns, but plenty of room to recover from mistakes, and a fluffy landing below to accept head-plants. It took an afternoon of practice to get the pedal-jump working. That was kindergarten.

First grade was Nitze's Couloir, 2,000 feet long and 45 degrees steep. The snow was windpacked, smooth and consistent, and while the couloir started off narrow—about 10 feet wide—it opened out gradually like a cornucopia. Falling would mean a long, fast slide, but no pinballing off rocks. "It's safe," said Gaimard. "Let's go."

"Because the snow was firm," says Seth, "I found the skiing easy and exhilarating. It seemed pointless to come to a complete stop on every turn, so I skied continuously, arcing out as the couloir widened into neat C-turns. But when I stopped, after a 1,500-foot rush, Gaimard scolded me. 'You must stop on every turn!' he said. 'You must control your speed and test the snow. If you ski like that on steeper terrain you'll lose control completely! If you don't prove to me that you have the confidence and skills to move on, we don't move up to the steeper, narrower couloirs.'

"The next day we climbed to the north couloir of the Aiguille Grive. Protected from the sun, the snow here was softer and drier than the east-facing Nitze's. The couloir was also narrower—about 8 feet wide, continuously, for about 300 feet. Then the rock walls ended as the couloir opened out into a broad slope. But falling was out of the question: there were sharp rocks in the middle of the couloir. I hit one, buried under the loose snow, and it took my ski away. I slid, head first, gaining speed on the 50-degree plunge. Gaimard waded out into the middle of the couloir to stop me, sinking his poles deep in the snow and leaning on them, hard. I smashed into this barricade, busting Gaimard's sunglasses. Much sobered, I retrieved my rock-speared ski and proceeded, slowly, stopping as ordered to test the snow on every turn.

"Graduation was another east-facing, hard-packed couloir, a nameless one leading off the summit of the Aiguille Rouge onto a glacier 2,000 feet below. At 50 degrees, with firm snow, it looked easier than the Aiguille Grive, but was much more dangerous because it funneled down to a 10-foot rocky neck 1,000 feet below the top. If you fell, you'd rocket on that firm surface and end as hamburger against the rock walls."

"You understand—you must not fall here," Gaimard said. "And do not stop until you are below the neck and safely to one side. If there is an avalanche, it all goes through there, and you will be flushed right down the toilet."

"But on that surface," says Seth, "the pedal-jump made the descent as routine as anything can be when your life is at stake. Time slowed down, and there seemed to be long moments, as I hung in the air, when I felt I could reach out with my edges for the next perch."

The masters of time dilation are skiers who can go 125 mph on skis. In Portillo, Chile, Franz Weber, then the world speed-record holder, prepared to attempt a new record. Son of an Austrian butcher, Weber, now living in Reno, is big, muscular and lantern-jawed, with a genial gap-tooth grin. He has gone 129.8 mph; that summer, as he coached a downhill race camp, he was training for another record attempt. At the top of the couloir where he hoped to set the track, Weber gestured at the slope falling away for a mile. "I can do one hundred and thirty-five miles per hour if I start right up against the rocks at the top," Weber said. If the sound of a downhiller at 80 mph is impressive, the sound of a human body passing at 50 mph faster is simply frightening. It's the same sound of tearing silk you hear when a jet fighter makes a low pass.

Speed-record skiers use special skis, 240 cm long, and skintight rubber suits. The helmets are aerodynamically shaped and smoothly faired to the shoulders. Steve McKinney, the previous record holder, built his helmets in the shape of a trout head, reasoning that the trout swimming upstream must have a pretty clean snout. Weber's helmet design is wide enough in front that he can tuck his hands in up under his chin, out of the airstream. To cut drag further, the skiers tape airfoils to the backs of their calves, and choose boots with no external buckles to generate turbulence. "At these speeds, air pressure lifts the skis right off the snow," Weber points out. "Stability is a problem. We are really flying on a thin cushion of air."

While the skier doesn't have far to fall, losing it at these speeds is painful. Snow is abrasive, and if you slide you burn: Weber has blistered the skin on his back, butt and shoulder, right through the rubber suit. If you tumble, however, you'll very likely break bones.

The speed record course starts as a steep couloir and is packed out smooth and hard by the racers. It takes several days, but noone wants to ski across bumps. The electronic timing lights are set up at what is judged to be the fastest point, where the course begins to flatten out at the bottom of the valley. Skiers start off low in the couloir, practicing their technique at lower speeds, and gradually move up. Each run is a bit faster; after each run the slower or less steady racers are eliminated as a safety measure. Only the strong skiers, those who are obviously prepared to go faster, move up the hill.

Around 110 mph a kind of dividing line is reached. "A lot of good skiers are strong enough to hold a reasonably stable tuck at one hundred miles per hour," Weber says. "At one hundred ten, very few can hold it together. At one hundred twenty, only half a dozen in the world can keep tucked in for the entire run. And any break from form at that speed slows you down immediately, or knocks you on your back."

It happened to Melissa Dimino. A slender dark-eyed racer from Squaw Val-

Franz Weber at high speed. Weber wears a skintight rubber suit, aerodynamically designed helmet, leg fairings, and tow-tipped 240 cm skis—all designed for low drag and stability at 130 mph.

ley, she was the only woman able to hold her tuck all the way through the timing trap at Les Arcs during the 1983 speed trials, and was rewarded with a new women's record, at 120 mph. But just beyond the trap she broke out of the tuck, lifting her shoulders. The wind slammed her onto her back and she literally scattered, skis and poles exploding away. Melissa walked to the helicopter for a trip to the hospital to get her lacerated arm stitched up.

Weber never did reach his 135 mph goal. The following winter saw a snow drought in South America, and the couloir never packed in. Then in 1985 he retired, his world record intact at 129.8 mph. He believed no one would go faster than that, but in the spring of 1987, four skiers came down the track at Les Arcs at higher speeds. Britain's Graham Wilke set the new record at 132.00 mph. "Even at one hundred twenty, we're already going faster than a skydiver can free-fall, even in a straight dive," Weber pointed out. The reason a skier can go faster is that he's cleaner, unencumbered by parachute and jump suit. But there is a point at which gravity will no longer overcome air resistance, and a limit to how smooth and slick the human body can be made.

Given enough strength, skill and courage, the only limit for the speed skier is physics.

Similarly, a jumper's distance is limited only by the size of the hill. Beyond 120 meters, ski jumps are called ski flying. FIS rules now forbid jumps beyond 191 meters (626.6 feet), but the unofficial record is held by Polish jumper Piotr Fijas at 194 meters (636.5 feet) on the ski-flying hill at Planica, Yugoslavia. At this distance, the skier is airborne for over seven seconds.

Skiing variations don't have to defy death. Adrenaline can be pumped just by trying out a new way to ski. Try a snowboard, which can glide swiftly through junk snow likely to trap a two-board skier. Snowboards look like miniature surfboards, and steer just as a surfboard or skateboard is steered. Jake Burton Carpenter builds his Burton Boards in Vermont, but travels to the deep wet snow of the high Sierra to find the best cruisin'.

"Anyone who has been on a skateboard can have fun on the board in his backyard," Carpenter says. "It's simple—you just stick your Sorel boots into the rubber straps on the board, pivot it

Invented by American surfers, monoskiing has caught on in a big way in France. The single wide ski works best in deep snow. *(Rossignol Ski Company/Chappaz)*

around to point downhill, and go. Steer it by edging." In the big mountains, snow surfers ride the surface just as they would the big waves, cutting under the curl of a cornice, slaloming through the trees, jumping hummocks and pipelining down gullies.

Midway between the snowboard and "real" skis falls the monoski, invented by surfer Mike Doyle. The monoski is just a big ski, wide enough for two sets of bindings side-by-side. It's great for powder skiing and junk snow, but very difficult to ski on hardpack. You obviously can't skate, stem or even walk on a monoski— to get up a lift ramp you have to kick one foot out of its binding and skateboard along. However, you can't very well cross your tips under the snow, either.

Like freestyle skiing and windsurfing, the monoski is an American invention over which the Europeans—particularly the French—have gone nuts. Rossignol, the world's largest ski manufacturer, sells several thousand of the things in France each year, and only a

The upskier uses a specially designed, hand-controlled nylon canopy to ski up slopes above tree line. He then carries the canopy in his pack while skiing back down the mountain. *(Robert Lienemann)*

few in America. That will change: mono-skis are being manufactured in the United States again, and most ski resorts now permit their use.

Upski is still another American invention, created by Coloradan Phil Huff, a pilot and hang glider. Upskiers use a parachute-like canopy to catch the wind for a free ride. With the wind at his back and the chute billowing 20 feet in front of his ski tips, the upskier rests against his harness as he zips across snowcovered lakes and meadows or gets a quick tow to the top of the mountain. Speed is controlled by spilling the wind through an adjustable vent in the center of the canopy. The upskier can carve turns at rocket speeds, like a waterskier, shoulder inches from the surface and ski edges throwing a rooster tail, or waltz along in easy crescent turns. Drop the control line, and the canopy deflates immediately to let a gust pass.

The large canopy means the Upski can't be used on a crowded lift-served mountain, or in the forest. It's for skiing above the tree line or in big open valleys. Learn to use the Upski in a gentle breeze, with an instructor to help you. Then you can become a snow sailor, free to ride the wind to the top of any hill, where you can stuff the Upski in its own fifteen-pound backpack and ride your skis back down.

(Bob Jonas)

13
The Pleasures of Total Skiing

Authors Seth Masia and Bob Jonas each remember a special time from their past ski seasons that underscores the pleasure of Total Skiing. For Bob it was a moonlit night at a backcountry hut.

"The trail to the hut was long; a storm had whipped falling snow into our faces all day. There was a feeling of closeness among us; our conversations that evening were far ranging, open and intimate. We read the poetry of Robert Service, and drank wine. As the night advanced, first one then another succumbed to a drowsy contentment. Then it happened.

"Suddenly, almost surrealistically, the interior of the hut was illuminated by moonlight through the dome. The shadows of tall pines were etched across the floor of the hut. My companion, Jef, and I looked at each other with excitement and stepped outside. The mountains were bathed in bright moonlight and the last of a bank of dark clouds was scudding off to the east.

"We dashed to the guide tent in excitement, feverishly putting on anoraks and windpants, boots and skis. Soon our shadows stalked us through the forest as we made for the crest of the nearby ridge. We climbed quickly on our skis; the cold was sharp in our chests.

"We stopped often to stare into the ethereal light of the moonlit night. Our excitement to get to the top, to ski down, became almost unbearable. At the crest of the ridge, we stared into the moon's full face, a brilliant pendant in an almost starless sky. Far below lay the white plain of a frozen lake. Towering at our backs were other mountain peaks, the hoary lords of the front range. The quiet was awesome.

"I raised my arms wide in salute as I glided straight down the slope, gaining speed. Dropping my arms, I came forward into a telemark, genuflecting deeply on one knee, as I slipped beneath flying powder. I had not experienced better powder in thirty-five years of skiing.

"On that mountain I became suspended in time, spiraling endlessly downward through fields of snow, light as air, in the silver light of the moon.

"We had to share the experience. We skied back to the hut and woke the others. We were exuberant, obnoxious, unrelenting—our friends must go out.

"Once out and on the mountain, the

effect spread like wildfire. Later, I looked up from the foot of the slope after a run to watch the other skiers ghosting down the mountain. Shouts of pure joy rang into the night.

"It was after one in the morning when sheer exhaustion overcame us. Atop the ridgecrest before one last run, my eyes swept the eastern horizon, gazing on the big peaks up the canyon, upon the ragged horn of the mountain above us. My vision became clouded. Tears were frozen to my lashes and cheeks. It was more than twenty below zero; it would fall to forty-two below before dawn. But that moment, I silently swore that in all the winters of my life, I would try to go high into the mountains during the December moon. I caromed drunkenly down the slope, falling often. It didn't matter."

For Seth, the pleasure of the Total Skier is best represented by the first real powder day one season. "It was the second week in December and I had been skiing on thin snow in northern Colorado," he recalls. "I was due in Vail to meet my friend Tom Lippert. As I drove down from Steamboat Springs late in the evening, new snow drifted across the road, and the temperature dropped into single digits. In Vail, Tom was waiting as arranged, drinking beer and telling lies with the guys from the ski patrol at Vendetta's. The patrollers invited us to start up the mountain with them at dawn.

"In the morning the snow lay a foot deep under the streetlamps in town, and it puffed into little clouds as we trudged through it toward the lower patrol headquarters. Brian McCarthy, the patrol leader, reported that the snow density was six percent, delightfully dry and feathery. As the sky brightened, we sipped hot sweet coffee and zipped up against the chill.

"We rode upward into low-hanging broken clouds, and emerged into sunshine near the top of the mountain. Here the clouds skirted around and about our shoulders. The snow had drifted up to three feet deep, and it still fell, sporadically, making dazzling sunshowers between the peaks.

"Brian sent us off with an avalanche control team. We pushed off into Sundown Bowl, along the ridge toward Never. This part of the mountain had not yet been opened to skiing for the season. The patrol checked the area after every new snowfall for avalanche potential. Today it was safe. The new snow was stable. C.J., the group leader, pointed to a steep line along the edge of a spinney of aspen, the blue-white snow surface billowed in gentle waves by the wind, and said 'Well, somebody go.'

"Tom blasted off and I followed, figure-eighting his tracks. In that bottomless light powder he quickly disappeared, hidden by the brilliant cloud of snow crystals blooming behind him. I stayed back half-a-dozen turns to keep out of Tom's cloud, and mirrored his perfect tracks, floating side to side in weightless rhythm. The snow boiled up my chest and over my shoulders, bracingly cold on the cheeks, caking against the bottoms of my goggles. Tom's cloud descended like an angel on an errand, sparkling in the sun, past the aspen grove, into the open, and straight for a stand of spruce.

"Figure-eighting, I followed the tracks. Behind, as we entered the woods, the patrollers whooped with glee. Where Tom's tracks looped left around a tree, I looped right, so our figure eights stitched the forest together, the trees standing like ornaments in the braids we wove.

"On the other side of the spruce, Tom waited, grinning and waving, covered with snow. 'Go, go, go!' he said.

"It was my turn to lead, and I wanted more trees. Without breaking rhythm I turned slightly toward another stand of spruce, thicker and darker, and slalomed through, ducking under branches in a couple of spots. Here the snow was drifted deeper still, protected from the wind. As the woods ended, as I plunged toward the sundrenched open snowfield and the cat track below, a deep drift lay in the lee of the stand. I blasted into it and the snow, shoulder deep, scattered like stars. Six more turns and I was on the road, panting, watching Tom and C.J. and two more red-coated patrollers weaving and chasing out of the woods like noisy pups."

For Seth and Bob, Total Skiing is a continuous adventure. Each season they make new discoveries.

You, too, can become a virtuoso of skiing, graceful in every technique, elegant gliding downmountain and overland, liquid in skiing the several states of snow. But Total Skiing is really more than acquiring exceptional skiing expertise. It has to do with not limiting yourself, with exposing yourself to a universe of possibilities.

The Total Skier draws from the three worlds of skiing—Alpine, cross-country and backcountry—a deep understanding of the sport and a great appreciation of natural beauty and variety in the human experience. Whether you're already a skier or a budding neophyte, uniting the three worlds of skiing will be more fun, rewarding and enjoyable over the course of a lifetime.

Appendix
A Sampler of
North American Skiing

NEW ENGLAND

Maine

Sugarloaf USA occupies a monadnock—a lone-standing mountain rising from the remote woods in the state's cold, forbidding center. The village is warm and cozy, the Alpine ski trails varied, the snow and weather typical of New England: when it's cold, it's very cold, but they can always make snow. Sugarloaf draws most of its skiers from Boston, because it's difficult to get to if you live anywhere else.

Near Sugarloaf, the Carrabassett Valley Ski Touring Center, the largest cross-country ski area in Maine, maintains 85 kilometers of groomed trails for all ability levels. In Baxter State Park, the touring skier will find miles of wilderness trails winding through dense spruce forests. In the middle of the park, imposing Mt. Katahdin offers heady free-heel descents when the snow is good.

New Hampshire

The premier Alpine resort in New Hampshire is Waterville Valley, a plush modern complex nestled between two hills: Mt. Tecumseh, where the big skiing takes place, and Snow's Mountain, the beginner area. Waterville is a full-service ski area, with cross-country skiing, swimming, tennis, conference rooms, and first-rate restaurants, all overseen by its creator, ex-Olympic skier Tom Corcoran.

North Conway is a town surrounded by medium-size Alpine ski areas of classic New England character. Just to the north is the Presidential range, centered on Mt. Washington, New England's highest peak, with the most forbidding weather in the lower forty-eight states. The ski areas are built at considerably lower elevations, and suffer less wind. Try Cannon Mountain and Wildcat north of town, or Mt. Cranmore right in the village. All are within a reasonable drive of the good hotels in town.

Skiers will find a myriad of groomed

cross-country tracks in New Hampshire's scenic White Mountains. The total kilometers is among the highest for a national forest in the U.S. The tracks originate from charming villages, old-world hotels and inns, and they interconnect on point-to-point routes. Among the most notable groomed systems are 100 kilometers at Bretton Woods, 65 kilometers at Waterville Valley and 142 kilometers maintained by the Jackson Ski Touring Foundation at Jackson.

Vermont

Vermont offers more skiing per acre than any state in the country. The big Alpine resorts are strung along Route 100, running down the spine of the state. Starting in the north:

Stowe is a classic New England village, and just a couple of miles out of town is Mt. Mansfield, Vermont's highest peak. Mt. Mansfield has great cruising terrain (try Nosedive) and some of the scariest steep runs anywhere (try any of the Front Four). Just over the hill is the smaller Smugglers Notch. Stowe's snowmaking is first-rate, its après ski varied and entertaining. Lodging runs the gamut from deluxe hostelries to tiny family-run lodges and even a state-run dormitory for hardy youngsters.

Twenty miles south is a north-to-south ridge harboring the Sugarbush complex and Mad River Glen. Mad River is Alpine skiing as it was thirty years ago: "natural snow" (that means no snowmaking) and challenging expert-level terrain. Sugarbush and Sugarbush North have developed into an ultramodern system with great snowmaking, high-speed lifts, a wonderful athletic club, comfortable condominiums and truly varied and in-

teresting terrain.

Another hour south brings the Alpine skier to Killington, a huge expanse covering several peaks, with five different base areas and a lift system so complex the trail map is superimposed over a topo map so you can find your way around. Killington's Bear Mountain claims the steepest continuous runs in the East, while its Snowshed area is home to the most progressive ski school in the country. Killington is the great place to learn to ski—they have it down to a science.

The town of Manchester lies near three excellent Alpine ski areas, all long on smooth intermediate runs: Bromley, Magic Mountain, and the giant in the area, Stratton. Stratton's runs are all long, consistent fall line skiing; there are plenty of hotels and condominiums within walking distance of the base lodge. The resort draws heavily on wealthy skiers from Connecticut.

Mt. Snow, in the south, was founded to draw inexperienced skiers from Boston and New York. Today, owned by Killington, the mountain has been developed largely for easy cruising. The trails are wide, gentle and long, the snowmaking excellent.

For the cross-country skiers intent upon backcountry touring, Vermont has put together the longest continuous ski trail in North America. Upon completion, the Catamount Trail will run 270 miles down the state from north to south. Along the way the tourer can change gear and track ski at some of the best-known tour centers in the east, all interconnected by the trail.

On the northern part of the trail, 105 kilometers of track link a variety of accommodations that range from the luxurious to the rustic in the Craftsbury area.

At Stowe the skier will find the Trapp Family Lodge, acknowledged as America's first touring center, with 1,700 acres criss-crossed by immaculately groomed trails that challenge skiers of all levels. Bolton Valley, just to the south, offers 100 kilometers of trail network.

Farther south, Mountain Top Cross-Country Resort features 40 kilometers of groomed track in some of Vermont's most scenic terrain.

THE EAST

New York

New York State has more alpine ski areas than any other state. The biggest is Whiteface, near the town of Lake Placid. In 1980, Whiteface was the site of the Winter Olympic Alpine events. The mountain gets plenty of snow; it offers good gentle beginner terrain and plenty of very challenging runs for experts. There is not much here, however, for intermediate skiers.

At Lake Placid the Mt. Van Hoevenberg Cross-Country Center features 50 kilometers of cross-country tracks that are built to Olympic standards. There are thirteen separate loops marked for beginners, intermediates and experts. Not far away the backcountry skier can enjoy state-maintained wilderness trails and telemark skiing while staying at the Adirondak Loj, which is surrounded by the largest wilderness in the east.

MIDWEST

Minnesota

There are probably more skis per household in Minnesota than any other state in the country. This is the heartland of cross-country track skiing. On Minnesota's northeastern tip, where the snow stays longer and is better, the track and tour skier can spend several weeks exploring an astounding variety of trails, 500 kilometers of which are regularly groomed, with lodgings linking many of the trails. Skiers can follow the beautiful North Shore Mountains Ski Trail above Lake Superior, and farther north, the Gunflint, Grand Marias and Grand Portage trails. The lodge-to-lodge program allows skiers to move from resort to resort on the trails while their luggage is transported by the lodging staffs.

At some locations, tourers can eschew the comfort of lodges and strike off to more rustic accommodations at remote huts.

At Biwabik, Minnesota, a great deal of energy—as well as enthusiastic support from the governor's office—has gone into creating the Giants Ridge Cross-Country Ski Resort. It has had a reputation as a world-class track racing center from the beginning, and attracts the elite of the racing world. The trails have been laid out with precision, and are well-groomed. There are challenging trails for competitors, and trails for the beginner, too.

Wisconsin

Wisconsin is home to the American Birkebeiner, the best-known cross-country track race in America. The 55-kilometer race runs from Hayward to Cable, and attracts citizen racers from throughout the U.S. and Europe. But the best time to enjoy the triple-width track circuits is not during "Birke week."

In northern Wisconsin, Eagle River Nordic is a popular destination cross-country resort featuring 60 kilometers of groomed trails, of which 25 kilometers are triple-width track.

THE WEST

Colorado

The premier state in the nation for skiing is Colorado. Colorado ski areas are high—summits go to 14,000 feet—and get frequent dry powder snow.

The biggest single-mountain Alpine complex is Vail, just two hours west of Denver on Interstate 70. Vail is huge, spread along a three-mile ridge line with 3,000 feet of continuous vertical along its length, plus four vast bowls on the back side of the ridge. Vail grooms its snow perfectly, owns the fastest lifts in the business, provides deluxe accommodations (all within walking distance of the lifts), and is easy to get to. No one has ever had a bad time in Vail. Little sister Beaver Creek, a ten-minute drive away, is worth a visit when Vail gets crowded, which isn't often now that the fast lifts are in. Cross-country skiers will find 25 kilometers of groomed trails at Beaver Creek, and over 40 marked backcountry trails on Golden Peak in Vail Village.

Closer to Denver—on the east side of Vail Pass—are the Summit County Alpine resorts. Copper Mountain, Breckenridge, and Keystone-Arapahoe are three separate complexes all within half-an-hour's drive of one another. Individually, each area is a respectable-sized resort. Taken together, they form a very sophisticated and varied community: Keystone, with long and gentle runs on its front side, ideal for beginners, and more advanced terrain in back, for racer training; Breckenridge, a rambling complex of slopes and bowls facing several exposures across two peaks, so you can follow the sun through the day; Copper, closest to Vail both geographically and in character of terrain, with a Club Med on site; and Arapahoe, where the dizzying steeps hold snow until midsummer. You can't ski from one area to another in Summit County, but if you stay there you can easily ski the different areas on succeeding days, and return to the ones you like best.

Steamboat, in the northern center of Colorado, is a great big honeybear of an Alpine mountain, with wide trails perfect for intermediate-level cruising. Steamboat does have some steep, expert terrain, but it offers something special for top-level skiers: the best tree skiing in the world. Vast areas like Priest Creek and Triangle offer soil conditions and exposure that encourage the spruce and aspen to grow just exactly far enough apart to shelter the new powder from wind and sun, while allowing skiers to make easy round turns. A powder day in Steamboat's trees is not to be forgotten. Steamboat is also very family-oriented—the town of Steamboat Springs began as a farming and ranching community, centered on family life, rather than as a raunchy mining town. So in Steamboat, there's plenty for kids to do, and they love the cowboy atmosphere the local ranchers still lend to the place.

Aspen is awesome—the town lies at the head of a valley that harbors four separate lift-served mountains, each of them vast. Rising from the center of town is Aspen Mountain, choice of most of the expert skiers and the place where the beautiful people—the ones who fly in in their own Lear Jets—choose to be seen. Just across Castle Creek is Aspen Highlands, the only area in town that offers locals a season pass. Because of that, here's where you'll find many of the hot-skiing youngsters and seasonal help from town. Buttermilk is a big beginner area, with gentle trails laid out so that new skiers can have a ski resort all to themselves. And Snowmass—after Vail, the biggest single-mountain complex in the Rockies—is a huge cruising mountain, with runs spread across four peaks. Aspen is a fascinating, multilayer society. Founded as a mining town, it's a charming Victorian place. The gaily painted frame houses and imposing stone hotels are home not only to local families and businesses, but to international importing companies, architectural and industrial design firms, financial and film investment organizations—and low-rent operations like the fictional Aspen State Teacher's College. Up on the hillsides live multimillionaires, and down-valley, in the trailer camps, live impecunious ski bums. The Aspen discos are wilder and more colorful than fashionable bars in New York and Los Angeles. A few years ago Aspen ran an advertising campaign that said: "Everything you've ever heard about Aspen is true." And it's true.

There are smaller Alpine resorts in Colorado that, if located anyplace else, would be considered major areas. The most notable of these are Crested Butte and Telluride. Both are old mining towns, difficult to get to and unbearably picturesque. Crested Butte is a single dramatic peak, named for its rocky crest. The runs facing town are wide and gentle, but there are some humdinger long steeps around back. Crested Butte was the cradle of modern telemarking, and on a typical day a large proportion of the skiers riding its lifts are locals on three-pin bindings. Telluride lies at the bottom of a box canyon, surrounded by 14,000-foot peaks. The ski hill looks awesome from town—all the runs descending the north-facing wall seem impossibly steep. All the intermediate terrain is around the corner, on the west-facing slopes. Both towns are well worth a visit.

Most of the Colorado Alpine resorts have well-groomed cross-country tracks and most of the track systems start at touring centers, with ski schools that handle all ability levels. At the Aspen Alpine complex there are 70 kilometers of tracks that in the future will connect the major Alpine mountains. The tracks follow the valley floors in the Roaring Fork and Castle Creek drainages. Most of the system is free to the public.

Twenty-five kilometers of track are up high (9,840 feet) at Vail's sister area, Beaver Creek. Skiers can enjoy spectacular vistas of the Gore range. There are also 25 kilometers at Copper Mountain.

The Elk River Valley in the Steamboat region has 60 kilometers of groomed track over four connected trail systems. Back in Steamboat, Sven Wiik, one of the fathers of western cross-country skiing, conducts lessons on tracks out of his Scandinavian Lodge near the base of the Alpine ski mountain.

Backcountry downhill, on both Alpine and downhill skis, is celebrated nearly everywhere in Colorado. Drive from Ouray to Silverton in the stunning San Juans and you will discover a hotbed of backcountry skiing. Most of the local devotees call Silverton home. The ascents are long, but the descents are among the most rewarding. It's no place for the casual backcountry skier, and avalanche hazard can be extreme.

Backcountry skiers in good condition will enjoy the tenth Mt. Division hut system being built between Vail and Aspen. Four huts are already in place, and as many as six more will be built. The distances between the huts range upwards of 12 miles and some of the descents are demanding. Skiers should have at least intermediate level Alpine ski experience. Just south of Aspen in the Castle Creek drainage lies the six-hut Alfred A. Braun system, which begins at the ghost town of Ashcroft at 9,500 feet. Most of the huts are above 11,000 feet, and skiers must be in good shape.

For skiers who want a challenging high-altitude backcountry tour with the convenience of lodging each night in a town or ski resort, there is the Colorado Grand Tour, a 90-mile route from St. Mary's Glacier on the Colorado Front Range to Vail's west slope. The route was first skied in its entirety in 1983. The trail is not well marked and requires a good nose for moving in the right direction in the far backcountry.

Utah

Utah claims to have "The Greatest Snow on Earth"—it even says that on the license plates now. The wind comes off the high desert out of Nevada, across the Great Salt Lake, and runs smack into the Wasatch range, dumping immense depths of snow so light you can almost breathe it. Alta, at the head of Little Cottonwood Canyon, just an hour from the Salt Lake City airport, has been famous for forty years as the powder skiing capital of the world. Years ago, dedicated skiers would hole up in the Alta Lodge, built fortresslike into the side of the canyon. There they could wait for the next storm, which was likely to close the road into the place, and after the weather cleared there was powder to be skied for days, until the road could be reopened and Salt Lake's local skiers could drive up to finish tracking the canyon out. Today Alta shares the canyon with the ultramodern Snowbird resort, widely admired for its broad, steep bowls. Both resorts are built strong against deep drifts and avalanche, but Alta retains the flavor of an old mining camp, while Snowbird looks like something out of *Star Wars*—it's a huge modern concrete complex. Stay at either place and pray for snow.

On the backside of the same range lies Park City, another mining town, with its mines still working beneath the ski lifts. Park City offers a wider variety of trails, from wide, smooth beginner to intermediate runs to the steep, deep glory of Jupiter Bowl. But one of the charms of Utah is that you can escape from Park City, skiing over the ridge behind Jupiter Bowl into Big Cottonwood Canyon (home of Brighton and Solitude), and thence on to Alta and Snowbird, via the Utah Interconnect. The Wasatch is one immense ski area, with these five resorts, plus Deer Valley and Park West, all backed up one against the other. You can stay in Salt Lake City and sample them all.

Perhaps the largest number of

skilled cross-country downhill skiers in the country call Salt Lake home. The reason is the powder snow of Big and Little Cottonwood canyons.

Tourers looking for an exotic adventure will not be disappointed in Bryce, Arches or Canyonlands national parks. Touring below nature's gothic arches, totems and silent mesas in the redrock sandstone deserts is beyond description.

Nevada

The Ruby Range, southeast of Wells, is high and dry . . . and increasingly popular with haute-route backcountry skiers and heliskiers looking for isolation, rugged terrain and great snow.

Idaho

Sun Valley is the first North American destination ski resort, the place skiers dream of retiring to. It's a total skier's mecca. And the annual Triple Crown Ski Race—track, telemark, Alpine giant slalom—is held here each year.

There are three lift-served mountains at Sun Valley. Two of them are low, their open terrain ideal for beginners and intermediates. The big mountain, famous Mt. Baldy, is laid out with long, wide trails descending in all directions. What sets the mountain apart from most others is that these trails are of astonishingly consistent pitch—there are no shelves or flat spots in them, just endless constant vertical. You can ski downhill two miles here, making uniform, rhythmic turns, and stop only when your legs can take no more. If you like Alpine

skiing nonstop, run after run, Sun Valley will quickly become your favorite resort.

Sun Valley's reputation was built as a cozy out-of-the-way retreat with great Alpine skiing, but it also features wonderful cross-country and backcountry skiing. The Wood River Valley at the toe of Baldy is laced with seven different groomed track systems. An eighth system is located at a working cattle ranch in the neighboring Sawtooth Valley. Altogether there are 140 kilometers of regularly groomed track.

The oldest heliski service in the country lifts Alpine and cross-country skiers into the soaring peaks of the Boulders and Pioneers above Sun Valley village. In these mountains and the contiguous Smokies and Sawtooths are located two different hut systems, as well as day huts.

The Sawtooth Haute Route is a classic and challenging backcountry Alpine route. But there is far more to tempt the backcountry skier. The Sawtooths and cross-valley White Cloud Peaks are a small part of the largest wilderness in the continental United States.

Wyoming

Jackson Hole is something else. Built on the flanks of the precipitous Teton range, it has the reputation of having the longest consistently steep Alpine runs in North America. Jackson is rightly regarded as the place for the expert's expert when it comes to Alpine skiing. Over the past decade the resort has developed a lot of intermediate terrain, somewhat diffusing that image, but Jackson remains a must on the visit list for any skier who aspires to excellence. Jackson Hole, with over 4,000 feet of vertical drop, is also the tallest Alpine ski area in the U.S.

Most of the snow in the Tetons falls on the Idaho side of the range. The little Alpine resort of Grand Targhee, situated at Alta, Wyoming, has the enviable reputation of having far more powder than packed skiing. The powder comes often and is deep; the place is a powder buff's nirvana.

A Jackson-based heliski service will get the powder skier everywhere else between Targhee and Jackson. Five Nordic tour centers operate at or near Jackson. And Yellowstone National Park is right next door.

Tourers can start from their lodge base at Old Faithful and follow trails down the Firehole River or move up the river to the Lone Star Geyser Basin. Snowcoaches take skiers into other sections of the park as well. When it gets cold—and temperatures below zero are rather common—the Dantesque steam clouds from the geothermal activity and the ice-bearded bison lend a fantasy aura to the park that is memorable. The far backcountry tourer may find elk isolated in geyser basins or in stream beds surrounded by six-foot snow banks. He may also find a hot springs bathing experience unlike anything else in North America.

Montana

Montana is a sprawling land of range and border mountains. The total skier can get away from it all at such hideouts as the Lone Mountain, Tobacco Root and Cross-Cut guest ranches. All the ranches are rich in western history and they look like the western ranch of America's imagination. You expect the cowpokes to come in off the range or up from the back forty. Out on the cross-country track you are surrounded by miles of empty land. Lone Mountain grooms 70 kilometers of track, while Tobacco Root and Cross-Cut groom 15 kilometers. Telemarking is popular at all the ranches, as long intermediate slopes abound.

New Mexico

The Southern Rockies have their own classic Alpine hill: Taos Ski Valley in New Mexico. The tiny village consists of half a dozen lodges, all run by expatriate Swiss and French, who compete fiercely in culinary arts—Taos is the gourmet's ski resort. The place is famous, too, for its steep trails and bowls, and for dry, light desert snow. Many of the runs are named for German anti-Nazis, because the resort's founder was evidently an operative for British Intelligence during World War II. Ernie Blake (it's not his real name, but a code name given to him by the British) is a colorful character, and he's created a colorful resort.

California

The biggest single-mountain complex in North America is California's Mammoth Mountain. Mammoth is the closest large Alpine ski area to Los Angeles, and every weekend tens of thousands of skiers leave the big city for the six-hour drive north across the Mojave Desert to the High Sierra. Mammoth can easily handle about 25,000 skiers on a good day—it has some of the most modern facilities in the world. It also gets unbelievable quantities of snow. Mammoth doesn't have a lot of vertical—not much more than 2,000 feet—but the summit is at nearly 12,000 feet, so the snow is excellent. And the terrain is vast. It's easy to get lost at Mammoth.

Three hours farther north—just 40 minutes from the Reno airport, or four hours from San Francisco—is Lake Tahoe, which no one who has seen it doubts is the most beautiful spot on earth. Like Mammoth, Tahoe's Alpine resorts get huge quantities of snow, though because they are lower (the summits are generally under 10,000 feet) the snow here is heavier and wetter. Squaw Valley, at the north end of the lake, offers the best steep skiing in the country—the runs are relatively short but they demand serious skills. Much of the terrain at Squaw is so steep that it would be considered too dangerous to open to the public at any other ski area in the country, but Squaw Valley skiers thrive on precipitous slopes. Neighboring Alpine Meadows offers some of the same type of terrain, but was developed more with families in mind, so most of the runs are gentler. Gentler still are the trails at Heavenly Valley, at the south end of the lake. Heavenly bills itself as the largest ski area in the country, a claim that will look like nonsense to anyone who has seen either Mammoth or Vail, but it is the only ski resort that bridges a state line: most of the trails are in California, but the good skiing is over on the Nevada side of the line. Heavenly is also unique in its lodging possibilities: you can stay at a big casino, watch big-time Las Vegas–style acts, and be on the slopes in just five minutes. Royal Gorge contains the largest single complex of cross-country tracks in the country, 62 trails spread out over 255 kilometers. Out on the tracks you will

find five warming huts, welcome stops if you are deep into the trail network and need a rest before returning to the stylish base lodge. Track skiers of all persuasions and skills will find a fun trail at the Gorge. And the Wilderness Lodge is an excellent place to stay.

Kirkwood is the other outstanding cross-country resort in the Tahoe region. Kirkwood grooms 75 kilometers of track over both flat meadow and rolling terrain. In the Central Sierra, Bear Valley Nordic and Tamarack Touring Center team up to create California's second largest destination cross-country resort; 125 kilometers of track link the two centers.

Backcountry huts are available at several California locations, but the Rock Creek system is probably the best known. Rock Creek huts offer spectacular scenery and easy access to the High Sierra. But getting to the base from which to start to the huts isn't easy. It's a 10-mile ski to the base lodge if you don't get a ride on the lodge's snowcat. Once at the main lodge or the huts, the scenery is breathtaking, and the downhill skiing on intermediate terrain seems limitless.

The Sierra Crest attracts backcountry skiers in April and May. There are a number of spectacular haute routes. Favorite trans-Sierra routes take skiers over Shepherd Pass and into the Mineral King Valley or the Tablelands above the Pear Lake Hut. The Redline is the highest and longest route down the range, continuing for 200 miles. That may be longer than any haute route in North America. The route is for expert skiers only.

Oregon

Bend, Oregon, is one of those western towns where community life revolves around skiing during the winter. Cross-country skiers will find a variety of some of the finest groomed track anywhere, all located at the Mt. Bachelor winter sports area. Expert trackmen from throughout the west converge on Mt. Bachelor Nordic Center's 50 kilometers of superb track for autumn and spring clinics. Racing is big here too. While beginners may find the trails tricky, there are enough trails for the neophyte to have a good time, and skiers can always step off-track and tour on miles of picturesque Forest Service trails.

The Three Sisters Wilderness, just down the road from the center, provides fine backcountry touring and cross-country downhill. Rounding out the ski experience is friendly lift-served Mt. Bachelor, 3,100 vertical feet of long, intermediate fall-line runs. The resort actually encourage free-heelers to use the lift facilities, a policy uncommon at most Alpine resorts. The snow falls often—there is a 16-foot average snowfall—and stays long at Bachelor. Bachelor is home to a number of cross-country and Alpine summer race camps.

Washington

While rain may dampen ski enthusiasm on the Seattle side of the Cascades, the Methow Valley, located on the east slope of the North Cascades, is considerably drier. The Methow Valley Ski Touring Association serves up a cornucopia of cross-country track skiing, 150 kilometers of interconnected trails linking several cross-country resorts along the Methow Trail which ranges up and down the valley from Twisp to Mazama. The gorgeous scenery alone is worth a visit to the Methow Valley. The mountains are big, the trails that follow the Methow River particularly appealing.

A three-hut system in the Rendezvous Hills above Winthrop is accessible to a wide range of skiing skills. A heli-ski service flies both cross-country and Alpine skiers into the stunning Liberty Bell country to complete the Methow Valley free-heel feast.

THE NORTH

Canada

Some of the grandest names in Alpine skiing lie north of the border. Mont Tremblant, north of Montreal, is one of the oldest and largest resorts in the East, and like Sun Valley in the West it set the pattern for much of the development to follow. Mont Tremblant, like most Eastern mountains, features relatively narrow trails cut through hardwood forests, and the snow tends to be on the firm side. But the layout here is easy to ski—the trails follow the fall line, they're long and consistent, and encourage rhythmic, nonstop skiing. And the Quebec atmosphere is unrelentingly charming.

The areas near Banff, Alberta—Lake Louise, Sunshine Village, and Norquay—provide good snow against the background of the astonishing Canadian Rockies. The views, especially at Lake Louise, are worth the trip. Louise is big, with a world-class downhill course any racing fan will want to follow. Sunshine offers easy, open-bowl skiing, largely above timberline. Norquay has a reputation for steep, challenging slopes.

British Columbia boasts two giant

resorts, back to back, within an hour's drive of Vancouver: Whistler and Blackcomb. The fog drifting in off the ocean brings these big areas plenty of snow, and when the weather lifts the gentle runs look endless; they are. The vertical here is immense, over 4,000 feet, and because the runs are, in general, fairly flat, you can ski for literally miles on the same run.

Heliskiing and the Canadian Rockies are nearly synonymous in the minds of skiers who love powder, whether Alpine or cross-country. The big heliski operators—Canadian Mountain Holidays, Mike Wiegele Helicopter Skiing and Mountain Canada—cover incredibly beautiful country in the Bugaboos, Cariboos, Monashees, Purcells and Selkirk ranges. Runs may be made on open slopes, glaciers or in the trees. While most single-run descents are between 2,500 and 3,500 vertical feet, they can range upwards to 8,000 vertical feet. The breadth of terrain skied in a day is usually limited to the strength of your legs.

In eastern Canada, track skiers will find a 125-kilometer network at the Far Hills Inn Ski Touring Center at Val Morin, Quebec. The popular Maple Leaf East Trail was originally cut by the legendary cross-country skier Herman "Jackrabbit" Johansen.

On the eastern end of Lake Superior near Sault Ste. Marie in Ontario, the Stokely Creek Ski Touring Center grooms 100 kilometers of impeccable tracks over a classic Nordic terrain of rolling wooded hills.

Alaska

Anchorage is the hub of skiing in Alaska. The programs there consistently turn out some of the best young track skiers in the nation. The city's sprawling bike trail system becomes a well-groomed track system during the winter months, much of it lighted to keep skiers moving beyond the brief daylight of the northern winter.

Down Turnagain Arm from the city is Mt. Aleyeska, one of a string of burly mountains rising straight up from sea level. Aleyeska's weather can be fierce. The skier may descend through a blizzard up top and be soaked by driving rains at the base. When the weather is good, the mountain features arresting views of Alaskan peaks and the ocean sweep of Turnagain Arm and Cook Inlet. The downhill skiing is some of the most demanding anywhere. Aleyeska is not a novice mountain.

If you go to Anchorage to ski, save time for Denali (Mt. McKinley). Skiers fly into McKinley out of the colorful little town of Talkeetna for an unforgettable backcountry tour in the Ruth Amphitheatre. Whether touring or downhilling, there are dramatic mountain landscapes wreathed in snow and ice. The Alaskan backcountry, especially in winter, transports one back to the wilderness frontier of the nineteenth century. There is a rawness and power that cannot be experienced anywhere else in the U.S. of A.